TRUE DISCIPLESHIP

This book is provided by the ministry
of Fred Kornis with Heartland
International Ministries. Please _PRAY_
for the grace, wisdom and resources
continually needed to stay on the
cutting edge in these strategic days.
THANK YOU! God bless you!

Fred Kornis-H.I.M.
P.O. Box 23
Shawnee Mission, KS 66201
USA

TRUE DISCIPLESHIP

WILLIAM MacDONALD

GOSPEL FOLIO PRESS
304 Killaly St. West, Port Colborne, ON L3K 6A6

TRUE DISCIPLESHIP
First printing 1962
This edition copyright © 2003
William MacDonald
All rights reserved

Abbreviations

KJV	King James Version
NASB	New American Standard Bible
NIV	New International Version
NLT	New Living Translation

The author of *True Discipleship* is no longer able to document some of the quotations in the book. If he is ever able to locate this information, it will be included in a subsequent edition.

Most short, one-sentence quotes are identified by author only.

Published by Gospel Folio Press
304 Killaly Street West
Port Colborne, ON L3K 6A6

ISBN 1-882701-91-7

ORDERING INFORMATION:
Gospel Folio Press
Phone: 1-800-952-2382
E-mail: orders@gospelfolio.com

Printed in the United States of America

CONTENTS

FOREWORD

*T*his book is an attempt to highlight some principles of New Testament discipleship. Some of us have seen these principles in the Word for years, but somehow concluded that they were too extreme and impractical for the complicated age in which we live. And so we surrendered to the chill of our spiritual environment.

Then we met a group of young believers who set out to demonstrate that the Savior's terms of discipleship are not only highly practical but that they are the only terms which will ever result in the evangelization of the world.

We acknowledge our indebtedness to these young people for providing living examples of many of the truths emphasized here.

To the extent that these truths are still beyond our own personal experience, we present them as the aspirations of our heart.

—WILLIAM MACDONALD

INTRODUCTION

$\mathcal{T}$he pathway to true discipleship starts when a person is born again. It begins when the following events take place:

- When a person realizes that he is sinful, lost, blind and naked before God.
- When he acknowledges that he cannot save himself by good character or good works.
- When he believes that the Lord Jesus Christ died as his substitute on the cross.
- When by a definite decision of faith, he acknowledges Jesus Christ as his only Lord and Savior.

This is how a person becomes a Christian. It is important to emphasize this at the outset. Too many people think that you become a Christian by living a Christian life. Not at all! You must first become a Christian before you can live the Christian life.

The life of discipleship outlined in the following pages is a supernatural life. We do not have the power in ourselves to live it. We need divine power. Only when we are born again do we receive the strength to live as Jesus taught.

Before reading any further, ask yourself the question, "Have I ever been born again? Have I become a child of God by faith in the Lord Jesus?"

If you have not, receive Him now as your Lord and Savior. Then determine to obey Him in all that He has commanded, whatever the cost may be.

One

TERMS OF DISCIPLESHIP

*T*rue Christianity is an all-out commitment to the Lord Jesus Christ.

The Savior is not looking for men and women who will give their spare evenings to Him—or their weekends—or their years of retirement. Rather He seeks those who will give Him first place in their lives.

> He looks today, as He has ever looked, not for crowds drifting aimlessly in His track, but for individual men and women whose undying allegiance will spring from their having recognized that He wants those who are prepared to follow the path of self-renunciation which He trod before them.[1]

Nothing less than unconditional surrender could ever be a fitting response to His sacrifice at Calvary. Love so amazing, so divine, could never be satisfied with less than our souls, our lives, our all.

The Lord Jesus made stringent demands on those who would be His disciples—demands that are all but overlooked in this day of luxury living. Too often we look on

11

Christianity as an escape from hell and a guarantee of heaven. Beyond that, we feel that we have every right to enjoy the best that this life has to offer. We know that there are those strong verses on discipleship in the Bible, but we have difficulty reconciling them with our ideas of what Christianity should be.

We can accept the fact that soldiers give their lives for patriotic reasons. We do not think it strange that Communists or Muslims give their lives for political or religious reasons. But that "blood, sweat, and tears" should characterize the life of a follower of Christ somehow seems remote and hard to grasp.

And yet the words of the Lord Jesus are clear enough. There is scarcely any room for misunderstanding if we accept them at their face value. Here are the terms of discipleship as laid down by the Savior of the world:

A Supreme Love for Jesus Christ

"If anyone comes to Me and does not hate his father and mother, wife and children, brothers and sisters, yes, and his own life also, he cannot be My disciple" (Lk. 14:26). This does not mean that we should ever have animosity or ill-will in our hearts toward our relatives, but it does mean that our love to Christ should be so great that all other loves are hatred by comparison. Actually, the most difficult clause in this passage is the expression, *"yes, and his own life also."* Self-love is one of the stubbornest hindrances to discipleship. Not until we are willing to lay down our very lives for Him are we in the place where He wants us.

DENIAL OF SELF

"If anyone desires to come after Me, let him deny himself, and take up his cross..." (Mt. 16:24). Denial of self is not the same as self-denial. The latter means foregoing certain foods, pleasures, or possessions. But denial of self means such complete submission to the lordship of Christ that self has no rights or authority at all. It means that self abdicates the throne. It is expressed in the words of Henry Martyn, "Lord, let me have no will of my own, or consider my true happiness as depending in the smallest degree on anything that can befall me outwardly, but as consisting altogether in conformity to Thy will."

> *My glorious Victor, Prince divine,*
> *Clasp these surrendered hands in Thine;*
> *At length my will is all Thine own,*
> *Glad vassals of a Savior's throne.* —H. G. C. Moule

A DELIBERATE CHOOSING OF THE CROSS

"If anyone desires to come after Me, let him deny himself, and take up his cross..." (Mt. 16:24). The cross is not some physical infirmity or mental anguish; these things are common to all men. The cross is a pathway that is deliberately chosen. It is, as C. A. Coates put it, "a path which so far as this world goes is one of dishonor and reproach." The cross symbolizes the shame, persecution, and abuse which the world heaped on the Son of God, and which the world will heap on all who choose to stand against the tide. Any believer can avoid the cross simply by being conformed to the world and its ways.

13

A Life Spent in Following Christ

"If anyone desires to come after Me, let him deny himself, and take up his cross, and follow Me" (Mt. 16:24). To understand what this means, one need simply ask himself, "What characterized the life of the Lord Jesus?" It was a life of obedience to the will of God. It was a life lived in the power of the Holy Spirit. It was a life of unselfish service for others. It was a life of patience and longsuffering in the face of the gravest wrongs. It was a life of zeal, of expenditure, of self-control, of meekness, of kindness, of faithfulness and of devotion (Gal. 5:22-23). In order to be His disciples, we must walk as He walked. We must exhibit the fruit of Christlikeness (Jn. 15:8).

A Fervent Love for All who Belong to Christ

"By this all will know that you are My disciples, if you have love for one another" (Jn. 13:35). This is the love that esteems others better than oneself. It is the love that covers a multitude of sins. It is the love that suffers long and is kind. It does not parade itself, is not puffed up. It does not behave rudely, does not seek its own, is not easily provoked, thinks no evil. It bears all things, believes all things, hopes all things, endures all things (1 Cor. 13:4-7). Without this love, discipleship would be a cold, legalistic asceticism.

An Unswerving Continuance in His Word

"If you abide in My word, you are My disciples

indeed" (Jn. 8:31). For real discipleship there must be continuance. It is easy enough to start well, to burst forth in a blaze of glory. But the test of reality is endurance to the end. Any man who looks back after putting his hand to the plow is not fit for the kingdom of God (Lk. 9:62). Spasmodic obedience to the Scriptures will not do. Christ wants those who will follow Him in constant, unquestioning obedience.

> *Keep me from turning back.*
> *The handles of my plow with tears are wet,*
> *The shears with rust are spoiled, and yet, and yet,*
> *My God! My God! Keep me from turning back.*
> —Author Unknown

A FORSAKING OF ALL TO FOLLOW HIM

"So likewise, whoever of you does not forsake all that he has cannot be My disciple" (Lk. 14:33). This is perhaps the most unpopular of all Christ's terms of discipleship, and may well prove to be the most unpopular verse in the Bible. Clever theologians can give you a thousand reasons why it does not mean what it says, but simple disciples drink it down eagerly, assuming that the Lord Jesus knew what He was saying. What is meant by forsaking all? It means an abandonment of all one's material possessions that are not absolutely essential and that could be used in the spread of the gospel. The man who forsakes all does not become a shiftless loafer; he works hard to provide for the current necessities of his family and himself. But since the passion of his life is to advance the

15

cause of Christ, he invests everything above current needs in the work of the Lord and leaves the future with God. In seeking first the kingdom of God and His righteousness, he believes that he will never lack food and clothing. He cannot conscientiously hold on to surplus funds when souls are perishing for want of the gospel. He does not want to waste his life accumulating riches that will fall into the devil's hands when Christ returns for His saints. He wants to obey the Lord's injunction against laying up treasure on earth. In forsaking all, he says with David Livingstone, "It's a pity I don't have more to give."

These then are the seven terms of Christian discipleship. They are clear and unequivocal. The writer realizes that in the act of setting them forth, he has condemned himself as an unprofitable servant. But shall the truth of God be forever suppressed because of the failure of God's people? Is it not true that the message is always greater than the messenger? Is it not proper that God be true and every man a liar? Should we not say with an old worthy, "Thy will be done though in my own undoing"?

Confessing our past failure, let us courageously face up to the claims of Christ upon us and seek from this moment on to be true disciples of our glorious Lord.

> *My Master, lead me to Thy door:*
> *Pierce this now willing ear once more.*
> *Thy bonds are freedom; let me stay*
> *With Thee to toil, endure, obey.* —H. G. C. Moule

Two

FORSAKING ALL

"So likewise, whoever of you does not forsake all that he has cannot be My disciple" (Lk. 14:33).

To be a disciple of the Lord Jesus, one must forsake all. This is the unmistakable meaning of the words of the Savior. No matter how much we might object to such an "extreme" demand, no matter how much we might rebel against such an "impossible" and "unwise" policy, the fact remains that this is the Word of the Lord, and He means what He says.

At the outset, we should face these unbending truths:

Jesus did not make this demand of a certain, select class of Christian workers. He said, *"Whoever of you…"*

He did not say that we must simply be willing to forsake all. He said, *"whoever of you does not forsake…"*

He did not say that we must forsake only a part of our wealth. He said, *"whoever of you does not forsake all that he has…"*

He did not say that a diluted form of discipleship would be possible for the man who holds on to his treasures. Jesus said, *"he…cannot be My disciple."*

Actually, we should not be surprised at this absolute demand, as if it were the only such suggestion in the Bible.

Did Jesus not say: *"Do not lay up for yourselves treasures on earth, where moth and rust destroy and where thieves break in and steal; but lay up for yourselves treasures in heaven, where neither moth nor rust destroys and where thieves do not break in and steal"* (Mt. 6:19-20)?

As John Wesley justly said, "To lay up treasure on earth is as plainly forbidden by our Master as adultery and murder."

Did Jesus not say: *"Sell what you have and give alms"* (Lk. 12:33)? Did He not instruct the rich young ruler, *"Sell all that you have and distribute to the poor, and you will have treasure in heaven; and come, follow Me"* (Lk. 18:22)? If He did not mean exactly what He said, what then did He mean?

Was it not true of the believers in the early Church that they *"sold their possessions and goods, and divided them among all, as anyone had need"* (Acts 2:45)? And has it not been true of many of God's saints down through the years that they literally forsook all to follow Jesus?

Anthony Norris Groves and his wife, early missionaries to Baghdad, became convinced that "they must cease to lay up treasure on earth, and that they should devote the whole of a very substantial income…to the Lord's service."[1] Groves' convictions on this subject are set forth in his booklet, *Christian Devotedness*.[2]

C. T. Studd decided to give his entire fortune to Christ, and to take the golden opportunity offered him of doing what the rich young man had failed to do…It was simple obedience to the black and white statements of God's Word.[3]

After distributing thousands to the work of the Lord, he reserved the equivalent of $9,588. for his new bride. She was not to be outdone by her husband. "Charlie," she asked, "what did the Lord tell the rich young man to do?"

"Sell all," he replied.

"Well then, we will start clear with the Lord at our wedding." And off went the money to Christian missions.

The same spirit of devotedness animated Jim Elliot. He wrote in his diary:

> Father, let me be weak that I might lose my clutch on everything temporal. My life, my reputation, my possessions, Lord, let me loose the tension of the grasping hand. Even, Father, would I lose the love of fondling. How often I have released a grasp only to retain what I prized by "harmless" longing, the fondling touch. Rather, open my hand to receive the nail of Calvary, as Christ's was opened, that I, releasing all, might be released, unleashed from all that binds me now. He thought Heaven, yea, equality with God, not a thing to be clutched at. So let me release my grasp.[4]

Our infidel hearts tell us that it would be impossible to take the words of the Lord literally. If we forsook all, we would starve. After all, we must make provision for our own future and the future of our loved ones. If every Christian forsook all, then who would finance the work of the Lord? And if there were not some Christians who were wealthy, then how could the higher class of people ever be reached with the gospel? And so the arguments come pouring forth in quick succession—all to prove that the Lord Jesus could not have meant what He said.

The fact of the matter is that obedience to the Lord's command is the most sane and reasonable life and the one that yields the greatest joy. The witness of Scripture and of experience testifies that no one who lives sacrificially for Christ will ever suffer want. When a man obeys God, the Lord takes care of him.

The man who forsakes all to follow Christ is not a shiftless pauper who expects to be supported by his fellow Christians.

He is industrious. He works diligently for the supply of his current necessities and those of his family.

He is frugal. He lives as economically as possible so that everything above immediate needs can be put into the Lord's work.

He is foresighted. Instead of accumulating wealth on earth, he lays up his treasures in heaven.

He trusts God for the future. Instead of giving the best of his life to the building up of vast reserves for old-age security, he gives his best to the service of Christ and trusts Him for the future. He believes that if he seeks first the kingdom of God and His righteousness, he will never lack food and clothing (Mt. 6:33).

To him, it is unreasonable to accumulate wealth for a rainy day. He would argue as follows:

How can we conscientiously hoard extra funds when the money could be used right now for the salvation of souls? "*Whoever has this world's goods, and sees his brother in need, and shuts up his heart from him, how does the love of God abide in him?"* (1 Jn. 3:17).

> Again consider the important command, *"You shall love your neighbor as yourself"* (Lev. 19:18). Can we, with any truth, be said to love that neighbor as ourselves, whom we allow to starve, when we have enough and to spare? May I not appeal to any who have experienced the joy of knowing the unspeakable gift of God, and ask, "Would you exchange this knowledge…for a hundred worlds?" Let us not then withhold the means by which others may obtain this sanctifying knowledge and heavenly consolation.[5]

If we really believe that Christ's coming is imminent, we will want to put our money to use immediately. Otherwise we run the risk of having it fall into the devil's hands—money that could have been used for eternal blessing.

How can we conscientiously pray to the Lord to provide finances for Christian work when we ourselves have money that we are not willing to use for this purpose? Forsaking all for Christ saves us from hypocrisy in prayer.

How can we teach the whole counsel of God to others if there are areas of truth, such as this, which we have failed to obey? Our lives in such a case would seal our lips.

Clever men of the world set aside abundant reserves for the future. This is not walking by faith but by sight. The Christian is called to a life of dependence on God. If he lays up treasures on earth, how is he different from the world and its ways?

The argument is frequently heard that we must provide for the future needs of our families; otherwise we are worse than infidels. The following two verses are used to support this view:

> *The children ought not to lay up for the parents, but the parents for the children* (2 Cor. 12:14).
> *But if anyone does not provide for his own, and especially for those of his household, he has denied the faith and is worse than an unbeliever* (1 Tim. 5:8).

A careful study of these verses will show that they deal with *current necessities* and not with *future contingencies.*

In the first verse, Paul is using irony. He is the parent, and the Corinthians are his children. He did not burden them financially, although he had every right to do so as a servant of the Lord. After all, he was their father in the faith, and parents ordinarily provide for their children, not vice versa. It is not at all a question of parents' laying up for their children's future. The whole passage has to do with the supply of Paul's present needs, not his possible future necessities.

In 1 Timothy 5:8, the apostle is discussing the care of poor widows. He insists that their relatives are responsible to care for them. If there are no relatives or if they fail in their responsibility, then the local church should care for Christian widows. But here again the subject is present needs, not future necessities.

God's ideal is that the members of the body of Christ should care for the immediate needs of their fellow believers:

*It is a matter of share and share alike. At present your plenty
should supply their need, and then at some future date their plenty may supply your need. In that way we share with each other, as
the Scripture says, "He that gathered much had nothing over, and
he that gathered little had no lack" (2 Cor. 8:15, PHILLIPS).*

This subject is dealt with at greater length in chapter
eighteen, "The Case for Frozen Assets."

A Christian who feels he must provide for future needs
faces the difficult problem of knowing how much will be
enough. He therefore spends his life in pursuit of a fortune of some indefinite amount and forfeits the privilege
of giving his best to the Lord Jesus Christ. He gets to the
end of a wasted life and finds out that all his needs would
have been provided anyway, if he had just lived whole-
heartedly for the Savior.

If all Christians took the words of the Lord Jesus literally there would be no lack of finances in the Lord's
work. The gospel would go out with increased power and
in increased volume. If any particular disciple faced a
need, it would be the joy and privilege of other disciples
to share whatever they might have.

To suggest that there must be wealthy Christians to
reach the wealthy people of the world is absurd. Paul
reached Caesar's household while he was a prisoner (Phil.
4:22). If we obey God, we can trust Him to arrange the
details.

The example of the Lord Jesus should be conclusive in
the matter. The servant is not above his Master. George
Müller believed, "It ill becomes the servant to seek to be

rich, and great, and honored in this world where his Lord was poor, and mean, and despised."

Anthony Norris Groves wrote:

> The sufferings of Christ included poverty (2 Cor. 8:9). Of course, poverty does not necessitate rags and dirt, but it does involve the lack of reserves and of the means to be luxurious…Andrew Murray pointed out that the Lord and His apostles could not have accomplished the work they had to do had they not been actually poor. He who would lift up another must descend, like the Samaritan, and the infinite majority of mankind always have been and still are poor.[6]

People plead that there are certain material possessions that are necessary for home life. That is true.

People plead that Christian businessmen must have a certain amount of capital to carry on a business today. That is true.

People plead that there are other material possessions, such as an automobile, which can be used for God's glory. That too is true.

But beyond these legitimate necessities, the Christian should live frugally and sacrificially for the spread of the gospel. His motto, like Anthony Norris Groves', should be, "Labor hard, consume little, give much—and all to Christ."

Each of us stands responsible to God as to what it means to forsake all. One believer cannot legislate to another; each person must act as a result of his own exercise before the Lord. It is a tremendously personal matter.

If as a result of such exercise, the Lord should lead a

believer to a degree of devotedness hitherto unknown, there is no room for personal pride. Any sacrifices we make are no sacrifices at all, when seen in the light of Calvary. Besides all this, we only give to the Lord what we cannot keep anyway and what we have ceased to love.

Three

HINDRANCES TO DISCIPLESHIP

*A*nyone who sets out to follow Christ can be sure that many escape routes will loom up before him. He will be given numerous opportunities to turn back. Other voices will call to him, offering to cut inches off the cross. Twelve legions of angels stand ready to deliver him from the path of self-renunciation and sacrifice.

This is remarkably illustrated in the account of three would-be disciples who allowed other voices to take precedence over the voice of Christ.

> *Now it happened as they journeyed on the road, that someone said to Him, "Lord, I will follow You wherever You go." And Jesus said to him, "Foxes have holes and birds of the air have nests, but the Son of Man has nowhere to lay His head." Then He said to another, "Follow Me." But he said, "Lord, let me first go and bury my father." Jesus said to him, "Let the dead bury their own dead, but you go and preach the kingdom of God." And another also said, "Lord, I will follow You, but let me first go and bid them farewell who are at my house." But Jesus said to him, "No one, having put his hand to the plow, and looking back, is fit for the kingdom of God" (Lk. 9:57-62).*

Three unnamed men came face to face with Jesus

Christ. They felt an inner compulsion to follow Him. But they permitted something else to come between their souls and complete dedication to Him.

Mr. Too Quick

The first man has been called Mr. Too Quick. He enthusiastically volunteered to follow the Lord anywhere. *"Lord, I will follow You wherever You go."* No cost would be too great. No cross would be too heavy. No path would be too rough.

The Savior's reply at first seems to have no connection with the willing-hearted offer of Mr. Too Quick. Jesus said. *"Foxes have holes and birds of the air have nests, but the Son of Man has nowhere to lay His head."* Actually the Lord's answer was most appropriate. It was as if He said, "You claim to be willing to follow Me anywhere, but are you willing to do without the material comforts of life? Foxes have more of this world's comforts than I have. The birds have a nest they can call their own. But I am a homeless wanderer in the world My hands have made. Are you willing to sacrifice the security of a home to follow Me? Are you willing to forego the legitimate comforts of life in order to serve Me devotedly?"

Apparently the man was not willing, because we hear no more of him in the Scriptures. His love for earthly conveniences was greater than his dedication to Christ.

Mr. Too Slow

The second man has been called Mr. Too Slow. He did not volunteer, like the first man; rather the Savior called him to be a follower. His reply was not an outright refusal. It was not that he was completely disinterested in the Lord. Rather there was something he wanted to do first. This was his great sin. He put his own claims above the claims of Christ. Notice his reply, *"Lord, let me first go and bury my father."* Now it is perfectly legitimate for a son to show common respect to his parents. And if a father has died, it is certainly within the bounds of the Christian faith that he should be given a decent burial. But the legitimate courtesies of life become positively sinful when they take priority over the interests of the Lord Jesus. The real ambition of this man's life is exposed by his naked request, *"Lord,...me first..."* The other words he spoke were mere camouflage to hide his underlying desire to put self first.

Apparently he did not realize that the words *"Lord... me first"* are a moral absurdity and an impossibility. If Christ is Lord, then He must come first. If the personal pronoun "I" is on the throne, then Christ is no longer in control.

Mr. Too Slow had a job to accomplish, and he let this job have first place. It was therefore fitting that Jesus should say to him, *"Let the dead bury their own dead, but you go and preach the kingdom of God."* We might paraphrase His words as follows: "There are certain things which the spiritually dead can do just as well as believers. But there are other things in life which only a believer can do. See that you do not spend your life doing what an unconverted man could have done just as well. Let the spiritually dead bury the physically dead. But as for you, be indispensable. Let the main thrust of your life be to advance My cause on earth."

It seems that the price was too great for Mr. Too Slow to pay. He passes off the stage of time into a nameless silence.

If the first man illustrated material comforts as a hindrance to discipleship, the second might speak of a job or an occupation taking precedence over the main reason for a Christian's existence. It is not that there is anything wrong in secular employment; God's will is that man should work in order to provide for his needs and those of his family. But the life of true discipleship demands that the kingdom of God and His righteousness be sought first; that a believer should not spend his life doing what the unregenerate could do as well, if not better; and that the function of a job is merely to provide for current necessities while the main vocation of the Christian is to preach the kingdom of God.

MR. TOO EASY

The third man has been called Mr. Too Easy. He resembled the first in that he volunteered to follow the Lord. But he resembled the second in that he used those contradictory words, *"Lord...me first..."* He said, *"Lord, I will follow You, but let me first go and bid them farewell who are at my house."*

Once again we must admit that, taken by itself, there was nothing basically wrong with his request. It is not contrary to God's law to show a loving interest in one's relatives or to observe the rules of etiquette when leaving them. What then was the point on which this man failed the test? It was this—he allowed the tender ties of nature to supersede the place of Christ.

And so with penetrating insight, the Lord Jesus said, *"No one, having put his hand to the plow, and looking back, is fit for the kingdom of God."* In other words, "My disciples are not made of such self-centered, flabby stuff as you have exhibited. I want those who are willing to renounce home ties, who will not be distracted by sentimental relatives, who will put Me above everyone else in their lives."

We are forced to conclude that Mr. Too Easy left Jesus and walked sadly down the road. His over-confident aspirations to be a disciple had dashed themselves to pieces on the rocks of congenial family bonds. Perhaps it was a weeping mother who sobbed, "You'll break your mother's heart if you leave me to go to the mission field." We do not know. All we know is that the Bible graciously refrains from giving the name of this faint-hearted fellow who, by turning back, missed the greatest opportunity of his life and earned the epitaph, "Not fit for the kingdom of God."

SUMMARY

These then are three of the primary hindrances to true discipleship, illustrated by three men who were not willing to go all the way with the Lord Jesus Christ.

Mr. Too Quick—the love of earthly comforts.

Mr. Too Slow—the precedence of a job or occupation.

Mr. Too Easy—the priority of tender family ties.

The Lord Jesus still calls, as He has ever called, for men and women to follow Him heroically and sacrificially. The escape routes still present themselves, saying with solicitous words, "Spare thyself! Be it far from thee!" Few are willing to respond—

> *Jesus, I my cross have taken,*
> *All to leave and follow Thee,*
> *Naked, poor, despised, forsaken,*
> *Thou from hence my all shalt be;*
> *Perish ev'ry fond ambition,*
> *All I've sought, or hoped, or known,*
> *Yet how rich is my condition,*
> *God and heav'n are still my own.*
>
> *Let the world despise and leave me,*
> *They have left my Savior, too;*
> *Human hearts and looks deceive me—*
> *Thou art not, like them, untrue;*
> *Oh! while Thou dost smile upon me,*
> *God of wisdom, love, and might,*
> *Foes may hate, and friends disown me,*
> *Show Thy face, and all is bright.* —H. F. Lyte

Four

DISCIPLES ARE STEWARDS

*J*t was to the disciples that the parable of the unjust steward was spoken in Luke 16:1-13. In it, the Savior sets forth principles that apply to disciples of all time. After all, the disciples of Christ are essentially stewards, entrusted with the care of His property and His interests here on earth.

The parable bristles with difficulties. It seems to commend dishonesty and crookedness. But when understood in its proper light, it is laden with instruction of greatest importance.

The story in brief is this. A wealthy property owner had hired an employee to care for his business. In the course of time, the master learned that this employee was squandering his money. Immediately he demanded an audit of the books, then gave him notice that his employment would be terminated.

The employee realized that his future prospects were dismal. He was too old to do hard physical labor, and he was ashamed to beg. So he hit on a scheme that would assure him friends for the days ahead. He went to one of his master's accounts and asked, "How much do you owe my boss?" The answer was, "Seven hundred and fifty gallons of oil." "Well," said the employee, "pay for half that amount and we'll call it even." He went to another of his employer's debtors and asked, "How much do you owe?" The customer replied, "Eight hundred bushels of wheat." "I see; well, you pay me six hundred and forty bushels, and we'll consider the account closed."

Even more shocking than the action of the dishonest employee is the comment that follows:

> *And his lord commended the unrighteous steward because he had done wisely; for the sons of this world are for their own generation wiser than the children of light* (v. 8, RV).

How are we to understand this apparent approval of dishonest business practices? One thing is certain. Neither his lord nor our Lord commended such crookedness. It was this very thing that caused him to be dismissed in the first place. No righteous person could ever approve of such cheating and unfaithfulness. Whatever else the parable teaches, it does not suggest that embezzlement is ever justified.

There is only one thing for which the unjust steward could be commended, that is, that he planned for the future. He took steps to ensure that he would still have friends after his stewardship had ended. He acted for "then" instead of "now."

That is the point of the parable. Worldly people take forceful action to provide for the days ahead. The only future they are concerned about is their old age, their years of retirement. So they work diligently to make sure that they will be comfortably situated when they are no longer able to carry on gainful employment. No stone is left unturned in their quest for social security.

In this respect, the unsaved are wiser than Christians. However, in order to understand why, we must realize that the Christian's future is not on this earth but in heaven. This is the crucial point. The future for an unbeliever means the time between now and the grave. The future for a child of God means eternity with Christ.

The parable teaches then that many unregenerate are more wise and aggressive in preparing for their future on earth than many Christians are for theirs in heaven.

With this background, the Lord Jesus presents the practical application of the lesson:

> *I say to you, make friends for yourselves by unrighteous mammon, that when you fail, they may receive you into an everlasting home* (Lk. 16:9).

The mammon of unrighteousness is money or other material possessions. We can use these things for winning souls to Christ. People won through our faithful use of money are here called *"friends."* A day is coming when we will fail (either die or be taken to heaven by Christ at the Rapture). Friends won through the wise use of our material possessions will then serve as a welcoming committee to receive us into the everlasting dwelling places.

This is the way in which wise stewards plan for the future—not by spending their little lives in a vain quest for security on earth; but in a passionate endeavor to be surrounded in heaven by friends who were won to Christ through their money. Money that was converted into

35

Bibles, Testaments, Scripture portions, tracts, and other Christian literature. Money that was used to support missionaries and other Christian workers. Money that helped to finance Christian radio programs and other worthy Christian activities. In short, money that was used for the spread of the gospel in any and every way. "The only way we can lay up our treasures in heaven is to put them into something that is going to heaven."

When a Christian sees that his material possessions can be used in the salvation of precious souls, he loses his love for "things." Luxury, wealth and material splendor turn sour in his stomach. He longs to see the mammon of unrighteousness converted by divine alchemy into worshippers of the Lamb forever and ever. He is captivated by the possibility of doing a work in human lives that will bring eternal glory to God and eternal blessing to the people themselves. He feels something of the thirst of Samuel Rutherford, a Scottish preacher during the 1600s in the town of Anwo'th:

> O if one soul from Anwo'th
> Meets me at God's right hand,
> My heaven will be two heavens
> In Immanuel's land. —Anne Ross Cousin

To him all the diamonds, rubies, and pearls, all the bank deposits, all the insurance policies, all the mansions, pleasure boats, and magnificent cars are but mammon of unrighteousness. If used for self, they perish with the using, but if spent for Christ, they reap dividends throughout eternity.

The manner in which we deal with material things, the extent to which we grasp them, is a test of our character. The Lord emphasizes this in verse 10:

The man who is dependable in a very small matter is dependable also in a large deal; the man who is dishonest in a very small matter is dishonest also in a large deal (WILLIAMS' TRANS.).

Here the very small matter is the stewardship of material things. Those who are dependable are the ones who use these things for the glory of God and the blessing of their fellow men. Those who are dishonest are the ones who use their possessions for comfort, luxurious living, and selfish enjoyment. If a man cannot be trusted in a small matter (material things), how could he be trusted in a large deal (the stewardship of spiritual things)? If a man is dishonest with the mammon of unrighteousness, how can he expect to be faithful as a minister of Christ and a steward of the mysteries of God (1 Cor. 4:1)?

The Savior therefore presses the argument a step further: *"Therefore if you have not been faithful in the unrighteous mammon, who will commit to your trust the true riches?"* (Lk. 16:11).

Earthly treasures are not true riches; their value is finite and temporal. Spiritual treasures are true riches; their value cannot be measured and will never end. Unless a man is dependable in his handling of material things, he cannot expect God to trust him with spiritual prosperity in this life or treasures in heaven.

Again the Lord extends the argument by saying: *"And if ye have not been faithful in that which is another's, who will give you that which is your own?"* (Lk. 16:12, RV).

Material things are not our own; they belong to God. Everything that we possess is a sacred stewardship from God. All that can be called our own are the fruits of our diligent study and service here, and the rewards of faithful stewardship there. If we have not proved dependable in handling God's property, then we cannot expect to enter into the deep truths of God's Word in this life, or to be rewarded in the next.

With climactic emphasis, the Lord then summarized the teaching of the entire parable:

> *No servant can serve two masters; for either he will hate the one and love the other, or else he will be loyal to the one and despise the other. You cannot serve God and mammon* (Lk. 16:13).

There cannot be divided allegiance. A disciple cannot live for two worlds. A steward either loves God or loves mammon. If he loves mammon, he hates God.

And, mind you, this was written to disciples, not to the unsaved.

Five

ZEAL

A disciple can be forgiven if he does not have great mental ability. He can be forgiven also if he does not display outstanding physical prowess. But no disciple can be excused if he does not have zeal. If his heart is not aflame with a red-hot passion for the Savior, he stands condemned.

After all, Christians are followers of the One who said, *"Zeal for Your house has eaten Me up"* (Jn. 2:17). Their Savior was consumed with a passion for God and for His interests. There is no room in His army for half-hearted followers.

The Lord Jesus lived in a state of spiritual tension. This is indicated by His words, *"I have a baptism to be baptized with, and how distressed I am till it is accomplished!"* (Lk. 12:50). And again by His memorable utterance, *"I must work the works of Him who sent Me while it is day; the night is coming when no one can work"* (Jn. 9:4).

The zeal of John the Baptist was attested by the Lord when He said, *"He was the burning and shining lamp"* (Jn. 5:35).

The apostle Paul was a zealot. An unknown author has

tried to capture the fervency of his life in this sketch:

> He is a man without the care of making friends, without the hope or desire of worldly good, without the apprehension of worldly loss, without the care of life, without the fear of death. He is a man of no rank, country or condition. A man of one thought—the gospel of Christ; a man of one purpose—the glory of God. A fool, and content to be reckoned a fool for Christ. Let him be called enthusiast, fanatic, babbler or any other outlandish nondescript the world may choose to denominate him. But still let him be nondescript. As soon as they call him trader, householder, citizen, man of wealth, man of the world, man of learning, or even man of common sense, it is all over with his character.
>
> He must speak or he must die, and though he should die, he will speak. He has no rest but hastens over land and sea, over rocks and trackless deserts. He cries aloud and spares not, and will not be hindered. In the prisons, he lifts up his voice, and in the tempests of the ocean, he is not silent. Before awful councils and throned kings, he witnesses in behalf of the truth. Nothing can quench his voice but death, and even in the article of death, before the knife has severed his head from his body, he speaks, he prays, he testifies, he confesses, he beseeches, he wars, and at length he blesses the cruel people.

Other men of God have shown this same burning desire to please God. C. T. Studd wrote:

> *Some want to live within the sound*
> *Of church or chapel bell;*
> *I want to run a rescue shop*
> *Within a yard of hell.*

Incidentally, it was an article written by an atheist that spurred Studd to all-out dedication to Christ. The article was as follows:

> If I firmly believed, as millions say they do, that the knowledge and practice of religion in this life influences destiny in another, then religion would mean to me everything. I would cast away earthly enjoyments as dross, earthly cares as follies, and earthly thoughts and feelings as vanity. Religion would be my first waking thought, and my last image before sleep sank me into unconsciousness. I should labor in its cause alone. I would take thought for the morrow of eternity alone. I would esteem one soul gained for heaven worth a life of suffering. Earthly consequences would never stay my hand, or seal my lips. Earth, its joys and its griefs, would occupy no moment of my thoughts. I would strive to look upon Eternity alone, and on the immortal souls around me, soon to be everlastingly happy or everlastingly miserable. I would go forth to the world and preach to it in season and out of season, and my text would be, "What shall it profit a man if he gain the whole world and lose his own soul?"[1]

John Wesley was a man of zeal. He said, "Give me a hundred men who love God with all their hearts, and fear nothing but sin, and I will move the world."

Jim Elliot, martyr of Ecuador, was a torch of fire for Jesus Christ. One day, as he was meditating on the words, *"Who makes...His ministers a flame of fire"* (Heb. 1:7), he wrote in his diary:

> Am I ignitible? God deliver me from the dread asbestos of "other things." Saturate me with the oil of the Spirit that I may be a

flame. But flame is transient, often short-lived. Canst thou bear this, my soul—short life? In me there dwells the Spirit of the Great Short-Lived, whose zeal for God's house consumed Him. Make me Thy fuel, Flame of God.[2]

The last line was inspired from a fervent poem of Amy Carmichael:

> *From prayer that asks that I may be*
> *Sheltered from winds that beat on Thee,*
> *From fearing when I should aspire,*
> *From faltering when I should climb higher,*
> *From silken self, O Captain, free*
> *Thy soldier who would follow Thee.*
>
> *From subtle love of softening things,*
> *From easy choices, weakenings;*
> *Not thus are spirits fortified,*
> *Not this way went the Crucified,*
> *From all that dims Thy Calvary,*
> *O Lamb of God, deliver me.*
>
> *Give me the love that leads the way,*
> *The faith that nothing can dismay,*
> *The hope no disappointments tire,*
> *The passion that will burn like fire,*
> *Let me not sink to be a clod:*
> *Make me Thy fuel, Flame of God.*

The disgrace of the Church in the twenty-first century is that more zeal is evident among suicide bombers and cultists than among Christians.

In 1903, one man with seventeen followers began his attack on the world. His name was Vladimir Lenin. By 1918, the number had increased to forty thousand, and with that forty thousand, he gained control of the one hundred sixty million people of Russia. And though the movement has suffered setbacks in recent years, it still controls more than one-fifth of the world's population. However much one might be opposed to their principles, one cannot help admiring their zeal.

Many Christians felt strongly rebuked when Billy Graham first quoted the following letter, written by an American college student who had been converted to Communism in Mexico. The message today might be the language of terrorists. The purpose of the letter was to explain to his fiancee why he must break off their engagement:

> We Communists have a high casualty rate. We're the ones who get shot and hung and lynched and tarred and feathered and jailed and slandered, and ridiculed and fired from our jobs, and in every other way made as uncomfortable as possible. A certain percentage of us get killed or imprisoned. We live in virtual poverty. We turn back to the party every penny we make above what is absolutely necessary to keep us alive. We Communists don't have the time or the money for many movies, or concerts, or T-bone steaks, or decent homes and new cars. We've been described as fanatics. We are fanatics. Our lives are dominated by one great overshadowing factor: *the struggle for world Communism.*
>
> We Communists have a philosophy of life which no amount of money could buy. We have a cause to fight for, a definite purpose

in life. We subordinate our petty, personal selves into a great movement of humanity, and if our personal lives seem hard, or our egos appear to suffer through subordination to the party, then we are adequately compensated by the thought that each of us in his small way is contributing to something new and true and better for mankind.

There is one thing in which I am in dead earnest and that is the Communist cause. It is my life, my business, my religion, my hobby, my sweetheart, my wife and mistress, my bread and meat. I work at it in the daytime and dream of it at night. Its hold on me grows, not lessens as time goes on. Therefore, I cannot carry on a friendship, a love affair, or even a conversation without relating it to this force which both drives and guides my life. I evaluate people, books, ideas and actions according to how they affect the Communist cause and by their attitude toward it. I've already been in jail because of my ideas and if necessary, I'm ready to go before a firing squad.[3]

If Communists can be as dedicated as this for their cause, how much more should Christians pour themselves out in loving, glad devotion for their glorious Lord? Surely if the Lord Jesus is worth anything, He is worth everything. "If the Christian faith is worth believing in at all, it is worth believing in heroically" (Findlay).

"If God has really done something in Christ on which the salvation of the world depends, and if He has made it known, then it is a Christian duty to be intolerant of everything which ignores, denies, or explains it away (James Denney).

God wants people who are completely turned over to

the control of the Holy Spirit. These people will appear to others as if they were drunk with wine, but those who know better will realize that they are driven on by "a deep, enormous, haunting, never-sated thirst for God."

Let every would-be disciple take to heart the necessity of zeal in his life. Let him aspire to fulfill the description given by Bishop J. C. Ryle:

A zealous man in religion is pre-eminently a man of one thing. It is not enough to say that he is earnest, hearty, uncompromising, thorough-going, whole-hearted, fervent in spirit. He only sees one thing, he cares for one thing, he lives for one thing, he is swallowed up in one thing; and that one thing is to please God. Whether he lives, or whether he dies, whether he has health, or whether he has sickness, whether he is rich, or whether he is poor, whether he pleases man, or whether he gives offense, whether he is thought wise, or whether he is thought foolish, whether he gets blame, or whether he gets praise, whether he gets honor, or whether he gets shame, for all this the zealous man cares nothing at all. He burns for one thing; and that one thing is to please God, and to advance God's glory.

If he is consumed in the very burning, he cares not for it, he is content. He feels that, like a lamp, he is made to burn; and if consumed in burning, he has but done the work for which God appointed him. Such an one will always find a sphere for his zeal. If he cannot preach, and work, and give money, he will cry, and sigh, and pray. Yes, if he is only a pauper, on a perpetual bed of sickness, he will make the wheels of sin around him drive heavily, by continually interceding against it. If he cannot fight in the valley with Joshua, he will do the work of Moses, Aaron, and Hur, on the hill (Ex. 17:9-13). If he is cut off from working himself, he will give the Lord no rest till help is raised up from another quarter, and the work is done. This is what I mean when I speak of "zeal" in religion.[4]

Six

FAITH

*T*here can be no true discipleship without profound and unquestioning faith in the living God. He who would do exploits for God must first trust Him implicitly. Hudson Taylor wrote, "All God's giants have been weak men who did great things for God because they reckoned on God being with them."

Now true faith is always based on some promise of God, some portion of His Word. This is important. The believer first reads or hears some promise of the Lord. The Holy Spirit takes that promise and applies it to his heart and conscience in a very personal way. The Christian becomes aware that God has spoken to him directly. With utter confidence in the trustworthiness of the One who has promised, he reckons the promise as sure as if it were already fulfilled, even though, humanly speaking, it is impossible.

Or perhaps it is a commandment rather than a promise. To faith, there is no difference. If God commands, He enables. If He bids Peter to walk on the water, Peter can be sure that the needed power will be given (Mt. 14:28). If He commands us to preach the gospel to every creature, we can be sure of the needed grace (Mk. 16:15).

Faith does not operate in the realm of the possible. There is no glory for God in that which is humanly possible. Faith begins where man's power ends. George Müller explained, "The province of faith begins where probabilities cease and where sight and sense fail."

Faith says, "If 'impossible' is the only objection, it can be done!" C. H. Mackintosh put it this way:

> Faith brings God into the scene, and therefore it knows absolutely nothing of difficulties—yea, it laughs at impossibilities. In the judgment of faith, God is the grand answer to every question—the grand solution of every difficulty. It refers all to Him; and hence it matters not in the least to faith whether it be six hundred thousand (dollars) or six hundred million; it knows that God is all-sufficient. It finds all its resources in Him. Unbelief says, "How can such and such things be?" It is full of "hows;" but faith has one great answer to ten thousand "hows," and that answer is God.[1]

Humanly speaking, it was impossible for Abraham and Sarah to have a child. But God had promised, and to Abraham there was only one impossibility—that God could lie.

> [He], *contrary to hope, in hope believed, so that he became the father of many nations, according to what was spoken, "So shall your descendants be." And not being weak in faith, he did not consider his own body, already dead (since he was about a hundred years old), and the deadness of Sarah's womb. He did not waver at the promise of God through unbelief, but was strengthened in faith, giving glory to God, and being fully convinced that what He had promised He was also able to perform* (Rom. 4:18-21).

Faith, mighty faith, the promise sees
And looks to God alone;
Laughs at impossibilities
And cries, "It shall be done!"

Our God is the God who specializes in impossibilities (Lk. 1:37). There is nothing too hard for Him (Gen. 18:14). *"The things which are impossible with men are possible with God"* (Lk. 18:27).

Faith claims His promise, *"If you can believe, all things are possible to him who believes"* (Mk. 9:23), and exults with Paul, *"I can do all things through Christ who strengthens me"* (Phil. 4:13).

Doubt sees the obstacle,
Faith sees the way!
Doubt sees the darkest night,
Faith sees the day!
Doubt dreads to take a step,
Faith soars on high;
Doubt questions, "Who believes?"
Faith answers, "I."   —Author Unknown

Because faith deals with the supernatural and the divine, it does not always seem to be "reasonable." It was not using "common sense" for Abraham to go out, not knowing where he was going, but simply obeying God's command (Heb. 11:8). It was not "shrewd" of Joshua to attack Jericho without death-dealing weapons (Josh. 6:1-20). Men of the world would scoff at such "insanity." But it worked!

Actually, faith is most reasonable. What is more reasonable than that a creature should trust his Creator? Is it insane to believe in One who can neither lie nor fail nor err? To trust God is the most sensible, sane, rational thing that a man can do. It is no leap in the dark. Faith demands the surest evidence and finds it in God's unfailing Word. No one has ever trusted Him in vain; no one ever will. Faith in the Lord involves no risk whatever.

Faith truly glorifies God; it gives Him His proper place as the One who is completely trustworthy. On the other hand, unbelief dishonors God; it charges Him with lying (1 Jn. 5:10). It limits the Holy One of Israel (Ps. 78:41).

Faith gives man his proper place also as a humble suppliant, bowed in the dust before the sovereign Lord of all.

Faith is opposed to sight. Paul reminded us that *"we walk by faith, not by sight"* (2 Cor. 5:7). To walk by sight means to have visible means of support, to have adequate reserves for the future, to employ human cleverness in insuring against unseen risks. The walk of faith is the very opposite; it is a moment-by-moment reliance on God alone. It is a perpetual crisis of dependence on the Lord. The flesh shrinks from a position of complete dependence on an unseen God. It seeks to provide a cushion against possible losses. If it cannot see where it is going, it is apt to suffer complete nervous collapse. But faith steps forward in obedience to the Word of God, rises above circumstances, and trusts the Lord for the supply of all needs.

Any disciple who determines to walk by faith can be sure that his faith will be tested. Sooner or later, he will be brought to the end of his human resources. In his extremity, he will be tempted to appeal to his fellow men. If he is really trusting the Lord, he will look to God alone.

C. H. Mackintosh wrote:

> To make known my wants, directly or indirectly, to a human being, is departure from the life of faith, and a positive dishonor to God. It is actually betraying Him. It is tantamount to saying that God has failed me, and I must look to my fellow for help. It is forsaking the living fountain and turning to a broken cistern. It is placing the creature between my soul and God, thus robbing my soul of rich blessing, and God of the glory due to Him.[2]

The normal attitude of a disciple is to desire an increase in his faith (Lk. 17:5). He has already trusted Christ for salvation. Now he seeks to extend the areas of his life which are submitted to the Lord's control. As he faces sickness, trials, tragedies, and bereavements, he comes to know God in a new and more intimate way, and his faith is strengthened. He proves the truth of Hosea 6:3, *"Let us know, let us pursue the knowledge of the Lord."* The more he finds God to be trustworthy, the more anxious he is to trust Him for greater things.

Since faith comes by hearing and hearing by the Word of God, the disciple's desire should be to saturate himself in the Scriptures—to read them, study them, memorize them, meditate upon them day and night. They are his chart and compass, his guide and comfort, his lamp and light.

In the life of faith, there is always room for advancement. When we read of what has been accomplished through faith, we realize that we are like little children, playing at the edge of a boundless ocean. The exploits of faith are given in Hebrews 11. They rise to magnificent crescendo in verses 32-40:

> And what more shall I say? For the time would fail me to tell of Gideon and Barak and Samson and Jephthah, also of David and Samuel and the prophets: who through faith subdued kingdoms, worked righteousness, obtained promises, stopped the mouths of lions, quenched the violence of fire, escaped the edge of the sword, out of weakness were made strong, became valiant in battle, turned to flight the armies of the aliens. Women received their dead raised to life again.
>
> Others were tortured, not accepting deliverance, that they might obtain a better resurrection. Still others had trial of mockings and scourgings, yes, and of chains and imprisonment. They were stoned, they were sawn in two, were tempted, were slain with the sword. They wandered about in sheepskins and goatskins, being destitute, afflicted, tormented—of whom the world was not worthy. They wandered in deserts and mountains, in dens and caves of the earth.
>
> And all these, having obtained a good testimony through faith, did not receive the promise, God having provided something better for us, that they should not be made perfect apart from us.

A final word! We have mentioned that a disciple who walks by faith will doubtless be considered a dreamer or a fanatic by men of the world or even by other Christians. It is good to remember that "the faith that enables one to walk with God enables him also to attach the proper values to the thoughts of men" (C. H. Mackintosh).

Seven

PRAYER

The only completely satisfactory book that has ever been written on the subject of prayer is the Bible. All other treatments leave us with a feeling that there are depths that have not been reached and heights that have not been scaled. In this booklet, we cannot hope to improve on the efforts of others. All we can do is to summarize some of the important principles of prayer, especially as they have to do with the subject of Christian discipleship.

The best prayer comes from a strong inward necessity. We have all proved this to be true. When our lives are serene and placid, our prayers are apt to be dull and listless. When we reach a crisis, a moment of danger, a serious illness, or a heavy bereavement, then our prayers are fervent and vital. Someone has said that "the arrow that is to enter heaven must be launched from a bow fully bent." A sense of urgency, of helplessness, of conscious need is the womb from which the best prayers are born.

Unfortunately, we spend most of our lives trying to cushion ourselves from necessities. By the use of clever business methods, we provide comfortable reserves against every imaginable contingency. Through sheer human cleverness, we reach the stage where we are rich and increased with goods and have need of nothing. Then we wonder why our prayer life is shallow and lifeless and why no fire falls from heaven. If we truly walked by faith instead of by sight, then our prayer life would be revolutionized.

One of the conditions of successful prayer is that we must *"draw near with a true heart"* (Heb. 10:22). This means that we must be genuine and sincere before the Lord. There must be no hypocrisy. If we are to meet this condition, then we will never ask God to do something when we have it in our own power to do it. For instance, we will never ask Him to raise up a certain amount of money for a Christian project if we ourselves have surplus funds that could be used in this way. God is not mocked. He does not answer prayers if He has already given us the answer, and we are not willing to use it.

In the same connection, we should not pray for the Lord to send others on His errands if we are not willing to go ourselves. Thousands of prayers have been uttered on behalf of Muslims, Hindus, and Buddhists. But if all who prayed had been willing to be used by the Lord in reaching these people, then perhaps the history of Christian missions would have been more encouraging.

Prayer should be simple, believing, and unquestioning. It is all too possible to become absorbed with the theological problems connected with prayer. This serves only to dull the spiritual senses. It is better to pray than to solve all the mysteries connected with prayer. Let the doctors of divinity spin their theories concerning prayer. But let the simple believer storm the gates of heaven with childlike trust. It was Augustine who said, "The unlearned take heaven by force, and we with all our learning rise not above flesh and blood."

> *I know not by what methods rare,*
> *But this I know—God answers prayer.*
> *I know not when He sends the word*
> *That tells us fervent prayer is heard;*
> *I know it cometh soon or late,*
> *Therefore we need to pray and wait.*
> *I know not if the blessing sought*
> *Will come in just the guise I thought.*
> *I leave my prayers with Him alone,*
> *Whose will is wiser than my own.*   —Lola Henson

For true power in prayer, hold nothing back. Be surrendered to Christ. Go all out for Him. Forsake all to follow the Savior. The type of devotion that crowns Christ Lord of all is the kind that He loves to honor.

God seems to place a special value on prayer when it costs us something. Those who rise early in the morning enjoy fellowship with the One who likewise arose early to receive His instructions for the day from His Father.

Likewise, those who are in such deadly earnest that they are willing to pray through the night enjoy a power with God that cannot be denied. Prayer that costs nothing is worth nothing; it is simply a by-product of a cheap Christianity.

The New Testament often links prayer with fasting.

Abstinence from food can be a valuable aid in spiritual exercises. From the human side, it promotes clarity, concentration, and keenness. From the divine standpoint, it seems that the Lord is especially willing to answer prayer when we put that prayer before our necessary food.

Avoid selfish prayers. *"You ask and do not receive, because you ask amiss, that you may spend it on your pleasures"* (Jas. 4:3). The primary burden of our prayers should be the interests of the Lord. First we should pray, *"Your kingdom come. Your will be done on earth as it is in heaven."* Then we may add, *"Give us day by day our daily bread"* (Lk. 11:2-3).

We should honor God with great requests because He is a great God. Let us have faith to expect great things from God.

> *Thou art coming to a King,*
> *Large petitions with thee bring,*
> *For His love and power are such*
> *Thou canst never ask too much.* —John Newton

How often have we grieved the Lord by expecting so little of Him? We have been content with such scanty triumphs, with such poor attainments, with such feeble longings after higher things, that we have not impressed those around us with the thought that our God is a great God. We have not glorified Him in the eyes of men who know Him not by lives that arrested attention and awakened inquiry as to the power by which they were sustained. Too often it has not been said of us, as was said of the apostle, "They glorified God in me" (E. W. Moore).

In praying, we should first make sure we are in the will of God. Then we should pray, believing that He will hear and answer. *"Now this is the confidence that we have in Him, that if we ask anything according to His will, He hears us. And if we know that He hears us, whatever we ask, we know that we have the petitions that we have asked of Him"* (1 Jn. 5:14-15).

To pray in the Name of the Lord Jesus means to pray in His will. When we truly pray in His Name, it is the same as if He were actually uttering the request to God, His Father. *"And whatever you ask in My name, that I will do, that the Father may be glorified in the Son. If you ask anything in My name, I will do it"* (Jn. 14:13-14). *"And in that day you will ask Me nothing. Most assuredly, I say to you, whatever you ask the Father in My name He will give you"* (Jn. 16:23). *"Again I say to you that if two of you agree on earth concerning anything that they ask, it will be done for them by My Father in heaven. For where two or three are gathered together in My name, I am there in the midst of them"* (Mt. 18:19-20).

To ask, 'In His Name,' means to be taken by the hand and led to prayer by Him; it means, may I say, His kneeling by our side and His desires flowing through our heart. That is what it means: 'In His Name.' His Name is what He is, His nature, and therefore to pray in the Name of Christ must mean to pray according to His blessed will. Can I pray for evil in the Name of the Son of God? What I pray for should really be an expression of His nature. Can I do that in prayer? Prayer should breathe the power of the Holy Spirit, the mind of Christ, the desires of Christ in us and for us.

57

The Lord teach us more and more to pray in His Name. We should not think of closing a prayer, without the very words: 'In the blessed Name of our Lord,' but then the whole supplication should be infiltrated by, permeated by, the blessed Name of Jesus—all according to that Name" (Samuel Ridout).

If our prayer life is to be truly effective, we must keep short accounts with God. By that, we mean that sin must be confessed and forsaken as soon as we are conscious it has entered into our lives. *"If I regard iniquity in my heart, The Lord will not hear"* (Ps. 66:18). We must abide in Christ. *"If you abide in Me, and My words abide in you, you will ask what you desire, and it shall be done for you"* (Jn. 15:7). The person who abides in Christ stays so close to Him that he is filled with a knowledge of the Lord's will. He can thus pray intelligently and be assured of answers. Again, the abiding life demands that we obey His commandments. *"And whatever we ask we receive from Him, because we keep His commandments and do those things that are pleasing in His sight"* (1 Jn. 3:22). A right state of soul is necessary if our prayers are to be heard and answered (1 Jn. 3:20).

We should not only pray at certain stated times during the day; we should develop the attitude of prayer, so that we look to the Lord as we are walking along the street, driving in a car, working at a desk, or serving in the home. Nehemiah is a classic example of this spontaneous type of prayer (Neh. 2:4b). It is a good thing to *"[dwell] in the secret place of the Most High"* (Ps. 91:1) instead of making occasional visits there.

Finally, our prayers should be specific. It is only as we pray for definite matters that we can see definite answers.

Prayer is a marvelous privilege. By this means we can, as Hudson Taylor said, learn to move man through God.

> What ministries are in our hands for working miracles in the wonder realm of prayer! We can take sunshine into cold and sullen places. We can light the lamp of hope in the prison-house of despondency. We can loose the chains from the prisoner's limbs. We can take gleams and thoughts of home into the far country. We can carry heavenly cordials to the spiritually faint, even though they are laboring beyond the seas. Miracles in response to prayer! (J. H. Jowett).

To this, a writer named Wenham adds his testimony: "Preaching is a rare gift; prayer is a rarer one. Preaching, like a sword, is a weapon to use at close quarters; those far off cannot be reached by it. Prayer, like a breech-loader, has longer range, and under some circumstances is even more effective."

> *Lord, what a change within us one short hour*
> *Spent in Thy presence will prevail to make;*
> *What heavy burdens from our bosoms take,*
> *What parched grounds refresh, as with a shower!*
> *We kneel, and all around us seems to lower,*
> *We rise, and all the distant and the near*
> *Stands forth in sunny outline, brave and clear;*
> *We kneel, how weak! We rise, how full of power!*
> *Why, therefore, should we do ourselves this wrong,*
> *Or others, that we are not always strong,*

TRUE DISCIPLESHIP

That we are ever overborne with care,
That we should ever weak or heartless be,
Anxious or troubled, when with us is prayer,
And joy, and strength, and courage are with Thee?
                                    —Richard C. Trench

Eight

WARFARE

*O*ne could scarcely read the New Testament even casually without realizing that the figure of warfare is often used to describe Christ's program on earth. True Christianity is far removed from the hurdy-gurdy entertainment of modern Christendom. It is not to be confused with the luxury-living and pleasure-seeking that are so rampant today. Rather, it is a struggle to the death, an unceasing conflict against the forces of hell. No disciple is worth his salt who does not realize that the battle is drawn and that there is no turning back.

In war, there must be unity. It is no time for petty bickering, for partisan jealousies, for divided loyalties. No house divided against itself can stand. Therefore, the soldiers of Christ must be united. The way to unity is through humility. This is clearly taught in Philippians 2. It is impossible to have strife with a truly humble man. It takes two to make a fight. *"By pride comes nothing but strife"* (Prov. 13:10). Where there is no pride, there is no room for contention.

War demands austerity and sacrificial living. In wars of any consequence, there is invariably a vast system of rationing. It is high time that Christians realized that we are at war and that expenditures must be cut to a minimum so that as much of our resources as possible can be thrown into the struggle.

Not many see this as clearly as a young disciple named R. M. In 1960, he was president of the freshman class of a Christian school. During his term, it was proposed that expenditures be made for the usual class parties, jackets, and a class gift. Rather than approve such expenditures which did not contribute directly to the furtherance of the gospel, R. M. resigned from his post as president. The following letter was distributed to his classmates on the day his resignation was announced:

Dear Classmates:

Since the matters of class parties, jackets, and the class gift have been brought before the Cabinet, I, as the president of the class, have been considering the Christian attitude toward these areas.

I think we would find the greatest joy for our own selves in giving ourselves, our money, and our time entirely to Christ and for others, thus finding the reality of His words: "He who loses his life for My sake will find it."

For Christians to spend their money and time on things that do not result in a definite witness to the unbeliever or for the building up of His children in Him would seem to be inconsistent with the facts that 7000 people die daily from starvation and over half the world has never heard of man's only Hope.

How much more glory we could give to God by helping to spread the gospel to the other 60% of the world who have never heard of Jesus Christ or even in many neighboring homes instead of coming together in a little clique by ourselves, limiting our social well-roundedness to those of like mind, and wasting money and time for our own pleasure.

Since I am aware of specific needs and opportunities where finances can be used to such great advantage to the glory of Jesus Christ and for helping my neighbor here and abroad, it is impossible for me to allow class funds to be spent unnecessarily on ourselves. If I were one of those who are in so great a need, as I know so many to be in, I would want those who have the ability to do all that they could to supply me with the gospel and with my material needs.

"And as you wish that men would do to you, do so to them."

"But if anyone has the world's goods and sees his brother in need, yet closes his heart against him, how does God's love abide in him?"

Therefore it is with love and prayer, that you might see the Lord Jesus giving His all (2 Cor. 8:9), that I hereby submit to you my resignation as president of the class of '63.

In Him with you,

R. M.

War demands suffering. If young men today are willing to lay down their lives for their country, how much more willing should Christians be to lose their lives for Christ's sake and the gospel. A faith that costs nothing is worth nothing. If the Lord Jesus means anything to us at all, He should mean everything to us, and no considerations of personal safety or immunity from suffering should deter us in our service for Him.

When the apostle Paul sought to defend his apostleship against the attacks of his small-souled critics, he did not point to his family background or his education or his worldly attainments. Rather, he pointed to his sufferings for the sake of the Lord Jesus Christ.

> Are they ministers of Christ?—I speak as a fool—I am more: in labors more abundant, in stripes above measure, in prisons more frequently, in deaths often. From the Jews five times I received forty stripes minus one. Three times I was beaten with rods; once I was stoned; three times I was shipwrecked; a night and a day I have been in the deep; in journeys often, in perils of waters, in perils of robbers, in perils of my own countrymen, in perils of the Gentiles, in perils in the city, in perils in the wilderness, in perils in the sea, in perils among false brethren; in weariness and toil, in sleeplessness often, in hunger and thirst, in fastings often, in cold and nakedness—besides the other things, what comes upon me daily: my deep concern for all the churches (2 Cor. 11:23-28).

In delivering his noble challenge to Timothy, his son in the faith, he urged, *"You therefore must endure hardship as a good soldier of Jesus Christ"* (2 Tim. 2:3).

War demands implicit obedience. A true soldier will follow the orders of his superior without questions and without delay. It is preposterous to think that Christ could be satisfied with anything less. As Creator and Redeemer, He has every right to expect that those who follow Him into battle will obey His orders promptly and completely.

War demands skill in the use of weapons. A Christian's weapons are prayer and the Word of God. He must give himself to fervent, believing, persevering prayer. Only thus can the strongholds of the enemy be pulled down. Then, too, he must be proficient in the use of the sword of the Spirit, which is the Word of God. The enemy will do everything in his power to trick him into dropping this sword. He will cast doubts on the inspiration of the Scriptures. He will point to alleged contradictions. He will bring opposing arguments from science and philosophy and human traditions. But the soldier of Christ must stand his ground, proving the effectiveness of his weapon by using it in season and out of season.

The weapons of Christian warfare seem ridiculous to the man of the world. The plan that proved effective against Jericho would be ridiculed by military leaders today. Gideon's insignificant army would evoke derision. And what shall we say of David's slingshot, of Shamgar's ox-goad, and of God's paltry army of fools down through the centuries? The spiritual mind knows that God is not on the side of the biggest battalions, but rather that He loves to take the weak and poor and despised things of this world and glorify Himself through them.

War demands a knowledge of the enemy and of his strategy. So it is in the Christian warfare. *"For we do not wrestle against flesh and blood, but against principalities, against powers, against the rulers of the darkness of this age, against spiritual hosts of wickedness in the heavenly places"* (Eph. 6:12). We know that *"Satan himself transforms himself into an angel of light. Therefore it is no great thing if his ministers also transform themselves into ministers of righteousness, whose end will be according to their works"* (2 Cor. 11:14-15). A trained

Christian soldier knows that his bitterest opposition will not come from the drunkard, or the common thief, or the harlot, but rather from professed ministers of religion. It was the religious leaders who nailed the Christ of God to the cross. It was religious leaders who persecuted the early Church. Paul met his most savage attacks from the hands of those who professed to be God's servants. So it has been down through the years. Satan's ministers are transformed as the ministers of righteousness. They speak religious language, they wear religious clothes, and they act with an affected piety, but their hearts are filled with hatred for Christ and for the gospel.

War demands undistractedness. *"Everyone who serves as a soldier avoids becoming entangled in the affairs of civil life, so that he may satisfy the officer who enlisted him"* (2 Tim. 2:4, WEYMOUTH). The disciple of Christ learns to be intolerant of anything that might stand between his soul and complete devotion to the Lord Jesus Christ. He is ruthless without being offensive, firm without being discourteous. But he has one passion and one passion alone. Everything else must be brought into captivity.

War demands courage in the face of danger. *"Therefore take up the whole armor of God, that you may be able to withstand in the evil day, and having done all, to stand. Stand therefore..."* (Eph. 6:13-14a). It has often been pointed out that the armor of the Christian soldier in Ephesians 6:13-18 makes no provision for the back and therefore no provision for retreat. Why retreat? If *"we are more than conquerors through Him who loved us"* (Rom.

8:37), if no one can be successful against us because God is for us, if victory is assured before we ever start to fight, how can we ever think of turning back?

What though I stand with the winners,
Or perish with these that fall?
Only the cowards are sinners,
Fighting the fight is all.
Strong is my foe, who advances,
Snapped is my blade, O Lord;
See their proud banners and lances—
But spare me the stub of a sword.

—quoted by Amy Carmichael

Nine

WORLD DOMINION

*G*od has called us to world dominion. It was never His intention that we should be "born a man and die a grocer." It was not His purpose that we spend our lives as "minor officials in transient enterprises."

When He originally created man, the Lord gave him dominion over the earth. He crowned him with glory and honor and put all things in subjection under his feet. Man was clothed with dignity and sovereignty—just slightly lower than that of the angels.

When he sinned, Adam forfeited much of the dominion that had been his by divine decree. Instead of exercising undisputed sway, he ruled unsteadily over an uncertain realm.

In the gospel, there is a sense in which we can regain dominion. It is not now a matter of control over snarling dogs or poisonous snakes—rather, it is claiming the heathen for our inheritance and the uttermost parts of the earth for our possession. J. H. Jowett said, "True imperialism is empire by moral and spiritual sovereignty; allurement and dominion by the fascinating radiance of a pure and sanctified life."

Actually, this dignity of the Christian calling is something that Adam never knew. We are partners with God in the world's redemption. Dinsdale T. Young wrote, "This is our errand—to anoint men in the Name of the Lord to royalty of life, to sovereignty over self, to service for the realm."

The tragedy of much of life today is the failure to appreciate our high calling. We are content to spend our years "hugging the subordinate," or "majoring in minors." We creep instead of fly. We are slaves instead of kings. Few have the vision of claiming countries for Christ. Spurgeon was an exception. He wrote the following dynamic message to his son:

> I should not like you, if meant by God to be a missionary, to die a millionaire. I should not like it, were you fitted to be a missionary, that you should drivel down to a king. What are all your kings, all your nobles, all your diadems, when you put them together, compared with the dignity of winning souls to Christ, with the special honor of building for Christ, not on another man's foundation, but preaching Christ's gospel in regions far beyond?[1]

Another exception was John Mott, well-known missionary statesman. When President Coolidge asked him to serve as ambassador to Japan, Mott replied, "Mr. President, since God called me to be an ambassador of His, my ears have been deaf to all other calls."

Billy Graham told of a third exception: When the Standard Oil Company was looking in the Far East for a man, they chose a missionary to be their representative. They offered him ten thousand, and he turned it down; twenty-five thousand, and he turned it down; fifty thousand, and he turned it down. They said, "What's wrong?" He said, "Your price is all right, but your job is too small. God has called me to be a missionary."

The Christian's calling is the noblest of all, and if we realize it, our lives will take on new loftiness. We will no longer speak of ourselves as "called to be a plumber" or "called to be a physicist" or "called to be a dentist." Rather, we will see ourselves as "called to be an apostle (a sent one)" and all these other things as mere means of livelihood. We will see ourselves called to preach the gospel to every creature, to make disciples of all nations, to evangelize the world.

An immense task, you say? Immense, yes—but not impossible. But it calls for immediate and wholehearted action by every believer.

Think first of all of the world's population. There are over six billion people on earth today, and the rate of growth is dizzying. From the time of Christ it took 18 centuries to reach the one billion mark. A century later it had climbed to two billion. The total in the 20th century escalated to 4.4 billion. Now every three days the growth is equal to San Francisco's population.

One numerical outcome of this explosion of humanity is that there are twice as many people on earth now as there were in 1960. Another is that a tenth of all the people who have ever lived since creation are alive today.

In thinking of the urgency of world evangelism, we should keep in mind that while the life expectancy in developed countries is above 70 years, in the rest of the world it is below 40. Souls are sliding into eternity. There is no time to waste in sharing the gospel with them.

The Bible is central in world evangelization. *"Faith comes by hearing, and hearing by the word of God"* (Rom. 10:17). Of the more than 6,500 languages spoken globally, Scriptures exist in only about 2,500. The language used in many of these Bibles and Bible portions is outdated. It's like a foreign language to the people. Add to this the sad fact that 16 per cent of the population are illiterate; they couldn't read the Bible if they had one.

Western nations have not only religious freedom and gospel light; they also have massive resources. Christians who share in this are responsible to fuel world evangelization and alleviate human need with it.

A third of the world professes to be Christian, but this includes hordes of nominal ones. No one knows the exact number of evangelical believers. However, someone has ventured to estimate that if every true Christian shared the gospel with 40 unreached people, the world could be evangelized.

There are over a billion Roman Catholics and 217 million Orthodox members. Protestants number 351 million.

The fastest growing religion is Islam. Most of its 1.3 billion adherents are under 25. Fifteen countries are almost totally Muslim. Of the planet's 10,200 distinct religions, the other major ones are Hinduism, Buddhism, Atheism, Sikhism, and Judaism. Together they add another 1.4 billion to the total of souls without a Savior.

Communism is still an enemy of the Christian faith. It seeks to prevent one fifth of the world's population from hearing the truth in China, Cuba, Viet Nam, North Korea, and elsewhere.

Every member of every religion and philosophy is precious to the Lord Jesus. He died for each one. All should hear the gospel. The need is staggering.

How then is the world going to be reached for Christ with the gospel in our generation? The answer—only by men and women who love God with all their hearts and who love their neighbors as themselves. It is only the devotion and dedication that spring from an undying love that will ever accomplish the task.

Those who are constrained by the love of Christ will count no sacrifice too great to make for Him. They will do because of love to Him what they would never do for worldly gain. They will not count their lives dear unto themselves. They will spend and be spent if only men might not perish for want of the gospel.

> *Lord crucified, give me a heart like Thine!*
> *Teach me to love the dying souls of men—*
> *And keep my heart in closest touch with Thee;*
> *And give me love—pure Calvary's love*
> *To bring the lost to Thee.* —James A. Stewart

Unless love is the motive, the cause is hopeless. It profits nothing. The ministry then becomes nothing more than sounding brass or clanging cymbals. But when love is the guiding star, when men go forth aflame with devotion to Christ, no power on earth can stop the onward sweep of the gospel.

Picture then a band of disciples, utterly sold out to

Jesus Christ, driven by love for Him, traversing land and sea as heralds of a glorious message, tirelessly pressing on to new areas, finding in every life they meet a soul for whom Christ died, and coveting each one as a worshipper of the Savior throughout eternity. What method do these other-worldly men adopt in making Christ known?

The New Testament seems to present two principal methods of reaching the world with the gospel. The first is by public proclamation; the second is by private discipling (see, for example, Acts 20:20).

As for the first, it was used commonly by the Lord Jesus and by His disciples. Wherever people were gathered together, there was an opportunity for preaching the good news. Thus we find gospel meetings in the market places, in prisons, in the synagogues, on the beaches, and by the banks of rivers. The urgency and superlative character of the message made it unthinkable to limit it to conventional meeting places.

The second method of propagating the Christian faith is by private discipling of individuals. This is the method which the Lord Jesus used in the training of the twelve. He called this little band of men that they might be with Him and that He might send them forth. Day after day, He instructed them in the truth of God. He set before them the task to which they were appointed. He forewarned them in detail of the dangers and difficulties they would encounter. He took them into the private counsels of God and made them partners with Him in the glorious, yet arduous, divine plan. Then He sent them forth as sheep in the midst of wolves. Empowered by the Holy Spirit, they launched forth to tell the world of a risen, ascended, glorified Savior. The effectiveness of this method is seen in the fact that the band of disciples, reduced to eleven by the defection of the traitor, turned the world upside down for the Lord Jesus Christ.

The apostle Paul not only practiced this method himself but urged it on Timothy as well. *"The things that you have heard from me among many witnesses, commit these to faithful men who will be able to teach others also"* (2 Tim. 2:2). The first step is the careful and prayerful selection of faithful men. The second is the imparting to them of the glorious vision. The third is the sending forth of these men to make disciples of others (Mt. 28:19, ASV).

To those who lust for numbers and crave huge crowds, this method seems dull and tedious. But God knows what He is doing, and His methods are the best methods. More can be accomplished for God by a few dedicated disciples than by a great army of self-satisfied religionists.

As these disciples go forth in the Name of Christ, they follow certain basic principles which are outlined in God's Word. First of all, they are as wise as serpents, yet as harmless as doves. They draw on the resources of the Godhead for wisdom in the difficult path they have to tread. At the same time, they are meek and lowly in their contacts with their fellow men. None need fear physical violence from them; men need only to fear their prayers and their unquenchable witness.

These disciples keep themselves free from the politics of this world. They do not consider themselves as called to battle against any form of government or political ideology. They can operate under any form of government and be loyal to that government up to the point where they are required to compromise their testimony or deny their Lord. Then they refuse to obey and submit to the consequences. But they never conspire against a human government or engage in revolutionary tactics. Did not the Lord say in John 18:36, *"My kingdom is not of this world. If My kingdom were of this world, My servants would fight"?* These men are ambassadors of a heavenly country and thus pass through this world as pilgrims and strangers.

They are absolutely honest in all their dealings. They avoid subterfuge of all kinds. Their "yes" means yes, and their "no" means no. They refuse to adopt the popular lie that the end justifies the means. Under no circumstances will they do evil that good may come. Each one is an embodied conscience who would rather die than sin.

Another principle invariably followed by these men is that they anchor their work to the local church. They go out into the harvest field of the world to win converts to the Lord Jesus, but then they lead these converts into the fellowship of a local church where they can be strengthened and built up in their most holy faith. True disciples realize that the local church is God's unit on earth for propagating the faith, and that the best and most enduring work is built along these lines.

Disciples are wise to avoid entangling alliances of every kind. They steadfastly refuse to allow their movements to be dictated by any human organization. They receive their marching orders directly from headquarters in heaven. This does not mean that they operate without the confidence and commendation of Christians in their local church. On the contrary, they look upon such commendation as a confirmation of God's call to service. But they insist on the necessity of serving Christ in obedience to His Word and to His guidance for them.

Finally, these disciples avoid publicity. They try to keep themselves in the background. Their purpose is to glorify Christ and to make Him known. They are not seeking great things for themselves. Neither do they want to reveal their strategy to the enemy. So they work on quietly and unostentatiously, oblivious of man's praise or blame. They know that "heaven will be the best and safest place to learn the results of their labor."

Ten

DISCIPLESHIP AND MARRIAGE

"There are eunuchs who have made themselves eunuchs for the kingdom of heaven's sake. He who is able to accept it, let him accept it" (Mt. 19:12).

One of the major questions to be faced by every disciple is whether God has called him to married life or to celibacy. This is entirely a matter of individual guidance from the Lord. No one can legislate for another, and to interfere in such a vital sphere is a perilous business.

The general teaching of the Word of God is that marriage was instituted by God for the human race, with several purposes in mind:

It was ordained for companionship and pleasure. God saw, *"It is not good that man should be alone"* (Gen. 2:18).

It was designed for the procreation of the race. This is indicated by the Lord's command, *"Be fruitful and multiply"* (Gen. 1:28).

It was arranged for the preservation of purity in the family and in society. *"Because of sexual immorality, let each man have his own wife..."* (1 Cor. 7:2). There is nothing in the Word of God to suggest that marriage is incompatible with a life of purity, devotion and service for Christ. Rather we are reminded that *"marriage is honorable among all, and the bed undefiled"* (Heb. 13:4a). The record stands that *"he who finds a wife finds a good thing"* (Prov. 18:22). The Preacher's words can often be applied to marriage, *"two are better than one"* (Eccl. 4:9), particularly if the two are joined together in service for the Lord. The increased effectiveness of united action is suggested by Deuteronomy 32:30, where one chases a thousand, and two put ten thousand to flight.

And yet although marriage is God's will for the race in general, it is not necessarily His will for every individual. While it may be looked upon as an inalienable right, the disciple of the Lord Jesus may choose to forego that right in order to give himself more undistractedly to the service of Christ.

The Lord Jesus noted that in His kingdom there would be those who would become, as it were, eunuchs for His sake: *"There are eunuchs who were born thus from their mother's womb, and there are eunuchs who were made eunuchs by men, and there are eunuchs who have made themselves eunuchs for the kingdom of heaven's sake. He who is able to accept it, let him accept it."* (Mt. 19:12).

This is definitely a voluntary vow which a person takes as a result of two factors:

1. A sense of the guidance of God to be unmarried.
2. A desire to give himself more wholly to the work of the Lord without the added responsibilities of family life.

There must be the conviction of divine call (1 Cor. 7:7b). Only by this can the disciple be assured that the

Lord will give the needed grace for continence.

It must be voluntary. Wherever celibacy is a matter of ecclesiastical compulsion, the danger of impurity and immorality is great.

The apostle Paul emphasized the fact that an unmarried person can often give himself more fully to the King's business: *"He who is unmarried cares for the things of the Lord—how he may please the Lord. But he who is married cares about the things of the world—how he may please his wife"* (1 Cor. 7:32-33).

For that reason, he expressed the wish that the unmarried and widow should remain as he was, that is, unmarried (1 Cor. 7:7-8).

Even for those who were already married, the apostle insisted that the shortness of the time demanded that everything should be subordinated to the great task of making Christ known:

> But this I say, brethren, the time is short, so that from now on even those who have wives should be as though they had none, those who weep as though they did not weep, those who rejoice as though they did not rejoice, those who buy as though they did not possess, and those who use this world as not misusing it. For the form of this world is passing away (1 Cor. 7:29-31).

This certainly does not mean that a man should repudiate his home responsibilities, abandon his wife and children, and sally forth as a missionary. But it does mean that he should not live for the pleasures and satisfactions of home life. He should not use his wife and children as excuses for giving Christ second place.

C. T. Studd was fearful that his fiancee might become so occupied with him that the Lord Jesus would not have first place in her life. To avoid this, he composed a verse for her to recite daily:

> *Jesus, I love Thee, Thou art to me,*
> *Dearer than Charlie ever could be.*

The Communists have learned to subordinate family matters to the one great task of conquering mankind for their cause. Gordon Arnold Lonsdale is an example. After he was captured in England as a Russian spy in 1960, police found a letter from his wife and a six-page reply. His wife wrote,

How unjust is life. I fully understand you are working and this is your duty and you love your work and try to do all this very conscientiously. Nevertheless my reasoning is somehow narrow-minded in a female fashion, and I suffer dreadfully. Write to me how you love me, and maybe I will feel better."

Lonsdale replied, in part:

All I am going to say is that I myself have only one life and not an easy one at that. All I want is to spend my life so that looking at it, there will be no shame in looking back...I am 39 shortly; is there much left?[1]

"The time is short," wrote Paul, *"so that from now on even those who have wives should be as though they had none"* (1 Cor. 7:29).

The tragedy is that hasty or misguided marriage has often been the devil's tool to sidetrack a young disciple

DISCIPLESHIP AND MARRIAGE

from a pathway of maximum usefulness for Christ. Many aspiring pioneers have forfeited careers of undivided service for Him at the marriage altar.

Marriage may be a bitter enemy of fulfilling Christ's will that all should hear of Him.

> Marriage is God-given. But when it becomes a barrier to God's will, it is misused. We could name many—both men and women—who have had a definite call to the foreign field and never got there because associates held them back…Nothing—not even the God-given blessing of a lifemate—must hinder God's purpose for one's life…Today souls die without Christ because loved ones have taken priority over God's will.[2]

It is perhaps especially true in the case of pioneer workers that a life of celibacy is preferable.

> Men and women of the vanguard may need to deny themselves even the necessities of life to say nothing of its softer though perfectly legitimate pleasures. The duty of such is to endure hardness, to be good soldiers, unencumbered by the things of this life, athletes unentangled by any weight…It is a vocation, a calling, and an ordination to special service.[3]

For those who hear this call and answer, there is the proferred reward. *"Believe me,"* said Jesus, *"when I tell you that…every man who has left houses or brothers or sisters or father or mother or children or land for my sake will receive it all back many times over, and will inherit eternal life"* (Mt. 19:28-29, PHILLIPS).

Eleven

COUNTING THE COST

*T*he Lord Jesus never tried to coax men into a glib profession of faith. Neither did He seek to attract a large following by preaching a popular message.

In fact, whenever people began to swarm after Him, He would turn to them and sift them by setting forth the sternest terms of discipleship.

On one of these occasions, our Lord warned those who would follow Him that they should first count the cost. He said:

> *For which of you, intending to build a tower, does not sit down first and count the cost, whether he has enough to finish it—lest, after he has laid the foundation, and is not able to finish, all who see it begin to mock him, saying, "This man began to build and was not able to finish."*
>
> *Or what king, going to make war against another king, does not sit down first and consider whether he is able with ten thousand to meet him who comes against him with twenty thousand? Or else, while the other is still a great way off, he sends a delegation and asks conditions of peace* (Lk. 14:28-32).

Here He likened the Christian life to a building operation and to a war.

It is sheer folly to start building a tower, He said, unless you are sure you have enough funds to complete it. Otherwise the unfinished structure will stand as a monument to your lack of foresight.

How true! It is one thing to make a decision for Christ in the warm emotion of a mass evangelistic rally. But it is quite another thing to deny one's self, and take up the cross daily, and follow Christ. Although it costs nothing to become a Christian, it costs plenty to be a consistent believer walking in a path of sacrifice, separation and suffering for Christ's sake. It is one thing to begin the Christian race well, but it is quite another thing to slug it out, day after day, through fair weather and foul, through prosperity and adversity, through joy and through grief.

A critical world is watching. By some strange instinct, it realizes that the Christian life deserves everything or nothing. When it sees an out-and-out Christian, it may sneer, and scoff and ridicule—yet inwardly, it has deep respect for the man who recklessly abandons himself to Christ. But when it sees a half-hearted Christian, it has nothing but contempt. It begins to mock him, saying, "This man began to build, and was not able to finish. He made a big commotion when he was converted, but now he's very much like the rest of us. He started out at high speed, but now he's spinning his wheels."

And so the Savior said, "You had better count the cost!"

His second illustration concerned a king who was about to declare war on another. Would it not be sensible for him first to figure whether his 10,000 soldiers would be able to defeat the enemy's army which had twice the amount of soldiers? How absurd it would be if he should declare war first, then reconsider when the armies were marching toward each other. The only thing left would be to hoist the white flag, and to send out a surrender team, abjectly crawling in the dust, and meekly asking for terms of peace.

It is no exaggeration to liken the Christian life to war. There are the fierce enemies—the world, the flesh and the devil. There are discouragements, bloodshed, and suffering. There are the long weary hours of vigil, and the yearning for the light of day. There are tears and toil and testings. And there is daily death.

Anyone who sets out to follow Christ should remember Gethsemane, Gabbatha and Golgotha. And then he should count the cost. It is either an absolute commitment to Christ, or a snivelling surrender with all that that means of disgrace and degradation.

With these two illustrations, the Lord Jesus warned His hearers against any impulsive decisions to be His disciples. He could promise them persecution, tribulation and distress. They should first count the cost!

And what is the cost? The next verse answers the question: *"So likewise, whoever of you does not forsake all that he has cannot be My disciple"* (Lk. 14:33).

The cost is "everything"—all a man has and is. It meant this for the Savior; it cannot mean less for those who will follow Him. If He who was rich beyond all description voluntarily became poor, shall His disciples win the crown by some less costly means?

Then the Lord Jesus concluded His discourse with this summation: *"Salt is good; but if the salt has lost its flavor, how shall it be seasoned?"* (Lk. 14:34).

In Bible times, it seems that people did not have pure salt, such as we have on our tables today. Their salt had various impurities, such as sand, etc. It was somehow possible for the salt to lose its saltiness; the residue was insipid and worthless. It could not be used either as soil or fertilizer. At times it was used to make a footpath. Thus it was *"good for nothing but to be thrown out and trampled underfoot by men"* (Mt. 5:13).

The application of the illustration is clear. There is one main purpose of the Christian's existence—to glorify God by a life that is utterly poured out for Him. The Christian may lose his savor by laying up treasures on earth, by catering to his own comfort and pleasure, by trying to make a name for himself in the world, by prostituting his life and talents on the unworthy world.

If the believer misses the central goal of his existence, then he has missed everything. He is neither utilitarian nor ornamental. His fate is, like the savorless salt, to be trampled under foot of men—by their derision and contempt and scorn.

The final words are these: *"He who has ears to hear, let him hear!"* (Lk. 14:35).

Often when our Lord had uttered some hard saying, He added these words. It is as if He knew that all men would not receive them. He knew that some would try to explain them away, to dull the sharp edge of His cutting demands.

But He knew also that there would be open hearts,

young and old, who would bow to His claims as being worthy of Himself. So He left the door open! *"He who has ears to hear, let him hear!"* Those who hear are the ones who count the cost and still say:

> *I have decided to follow Jesus,*
> *Tho' no one joins me, still I will follow,*
> *The world behind me, the cross before me,*
> *No turning back, no turning back.*

Twelve

THE SHADOW OF MARTYRDOM

*W*hen a man is truly committed to Jesus Christ, it seems to be a matter of no importance to him whether he lives or dies. All that matters is that the Lord be glorified.

As you read *The Triumph of John and Betty Stam*, you will find a note repeated throughout the book— *"that...Christ will be magnified in my body, whether by life or by death"* (Phil. 1:20).

The same undertone is found in the writings of Jim Elliot. While still a student at Wheaton College, he wrote in his diary, "I am ready to die for the Aucas." Another time, he wrote,

> Father, take my life, yea, my blood if Thou wilt, and consume it with Thine enveloping fire. I would not save it for it is not mine to save. Have it, Lord, have it all. Pour out my life as an oblation for the world. Blood is only of value as it flows before Thine altar.[1]

It seems that many of God's heroes reached this same place in their dealings with God. They realized that *"unless a grain of wheat falls into the ground and dies, it remains alone; but if it dies, it produces much grain"* (Jn. 12:24). They were willing to be that corn of wheat.

This attitude is exactly what the Savior taught His disciples, *"Whoever desires to save his life will lose it, but whoever loses his life for My sake will save it"* (Lk. 9:24).

The more we think of it, the more reasonable it seems.

First of all, our lives do not belong to us anyway. They belong to the One who valued us with the cost of His precious blood. Can we selfishly cling to that which is Another's? C. T. Studd answered the question for himself when he wrote these words from Cambridge University in England in 1883:

> I had known about Jesus dying for me, but I never understood that if He died for me, then I didn't belong to myself. Redemption means buying back, so that if I belong to Him, either I had to be a thief and keep what wasn't mine, or else I had to give up everything to God. When I came to see that Jesus Christ had died for me, it didn't seem hard to give up all for Him.

Secondly, we are all going to die anyway if the Lord does not come in the meantime. Would it be a greater tragedy to die in the service of the King or as a mere accident statistic? Was Jim Elliot not right when he said, "He is no fool who gives what he cannot keep to gain what he cannot lose"?

Thirdly, it is unanswerable logic that if the Lord Jesus died for us, the least we could do would be to die for Him. If the servant is not above his master, what right do we have to go to heaven more comfortably than the Lord Jesus did? It was this consideration that prompted C. T. Studd to say, "If Jesus Christ be God and died for me, then no sacrifice can be too great for me to make for Him."

Finally, it is criminal to hug our lives when through their reckless abandonment eternal blessing might flow to our fellow men. Men often offer their lives in the interests of medical research. Others die to rescue loved ones from blazing buildings. Still others die in battle to save their country from enemy powers. What are the souls of men worth to us? Can we say with F. W. H. Myers:

> *Only like souls I see the folks thereunder—*
> *Bound who should conquer,*
> *Slaves who should be kings,*
> *Sharing their one hope with an empty wonder,*
> *Sadly contented with a show of things.*
>
> *Then with a rush the intolerable craving*
> *Shivers throughout me like a trumpet call—*
> *Oh, to save these! to perish for their saving,*
> *Die for their life, be offered for them all.*

Not all are required to lay down their lives as martyrs. The stake, the spear, the guillotine are reserved for a select few, relatively speaking. But each of us can have the martyr spirit, the martyr zeal, the martyr devotion. Each of us can live as those who have already abandoned their lives to Christ.

> *Come ill, come well, the cross, the crown,*
> *The rainbow and the thunder;*
> *I fling my soul and body down*
> *For God to plow them under.*
> —Author Unknown

Thirteen

THE REWARDS OF DISCIPLESHIP

A life that is abandoned to the Lord Jesus has its own deep reward. There is a joy and pleasure in following Christ that is life in its truest sense.

The Savior repeatedly said, *"He who finds his life will lose it, and he who loses his life for My sake will find it."* In fact, this saying of His is found in the four Gospels more frequently than almost anything else He said (see Mt. 10:39; 16:25; Mk. 8:35; Lk. 9:24; 17:33; Jn. 12:25). Why is it repeated so often? Is it not because it sets forth one of the most fundamental principles of the Christian life, namely, that life hugged for self is life lost, but life poured out for Him is life found, saved, enjoyed, and kept for eternity?

To be a half-hearted Christian can only insure a miserable existence. To be out and out for Him is the surest way of enjoying His best.

To be a true disciple is to be a bondslave of Jesus Christ and to find that His service is perfect freedom. There is liberty in the step of all who can say, *"I love my Master...I will not go out free"* (Ex. 21:5).

The disciple is not bogged down by petty affairs or by passing things. He is concerned with eternal matters, and,

95

like Hudson Taylor, enjoys the luxury of having few things to care for.

He may be unknown, and yet he is well known. Though constantly dying, yet he persistently lives. He is chastened but not killed. Even in sorrow, he is rejoicing. Although poor himself, he makes many rich. He himself has nothing, yet he possesses all things (2 Cor. 6:9-10).

And if it can be said that the life of true discipleship is the most spiritually satisfying life in this world, it can be said with equal certainty that it will be the most rewarded in the age to come. *"For the Son of Man will come in the glory of His Father with His angels, and then He will reward each according to his works"* (Mt. 16:27).

Therefore, the truly blessed man in time and in eternity is the one who can say with Bill Borden of Yale, "Lord Jesus, I take hands off, as far as my life is concerned. I put Thee on the throne in my heart. Change, cleanse, use me as Thou shalt choose."

> *"He was not willing that any should perish;"*
> *Jesus enthroned in the glory above,*
> *Saw our poor fallen world, pitied our sorrows,*
> *Poured out His life for us, wonderful love!*
> *Perishing, perishing! Thronging our pathway,*
> *Hearts break with burdens too heavy to bear:*
> *Jesus would save, but there's no one to tell them,*
> *No one to lift them from sin and despair.*
>
> *"He was not willing that any should perish,"*
> *Clothed in our flesh with its sorrow and pain,*

THE REWARDS OF DISCIPLESHIP

Came He to seek the lost, comfort the mourner,
Heal the heart broken by sorrow and shame.
Perishing, perishing! Harvest is passing,
Reapers are few and the night draweth near:
Jesus is calling thee, haste to the reaping,
Thou shalt have souls, precious souls for thy hire.

Plenty for pleasure, but little for Jesus;
Time for the world with its troubles and toys,
No time for Jesus' work, feeding the hungry,
Lifting lost souls to eternity's joys.
Perishing, perishing! Hark, how they call us;
Bring us your Savior, oh, tell us of Him!
We are so weary, so heavily laden,
And with long weeping our eyes have grown dim.

"He was not willing that any should perish;"
Am I His follower, and can I live
Longer at ease with a soul going downward,
Lost for the lack of the help I might give?
Perishing, perishing! Thou wast not willing;
Master, forgive, and inspire us anew;
Banish our worldliness, help us to ever
Live with eternity's values in view.

—Lucy R. Meyer

0

WHERE IS YOUR TREASURE?

The next six chapters by William MacDonald were originally published as a booklet. Because the contents are so closely connected with the subject of discipleship, it was decided to include them here.

Fourteen

WHERE IS YOUR TREASURE?

"*Do not lay up for yourselves treasures on earth...but lay up for yourselves treasures in heaven...For where your treasure is, there your heart will be also*" (Mt. 6:19-21).

The heart is where the treasure is. It can be in a safe-deposit box! Or it can be in heaven! But it cannot be in both places. Someone has said, "A Christian either leaves his wealth or goes to it."

The Lord Jesus forbade His followers to lay up treasures on earth. He wanted their hearts to be in heaven.

And yet this teaching of Christ seems radical and extreme to us today. Could He really have meant that? Doesn't common sense teach us that we should make adequate provision for our old age? Doesn't He expect us to be prudent and to set aside reserves for a rainy day? To care for our loved ones? These are serious questions, which should be faced squarely and honestly by all who profess to be followers of Christ.

What are the answers? What does the Bible teach with regard to wealth in the life of the believer? Is it wrong to build up a personal fortune? What is a Christian standard of living?

Fifteen

DILIGENT IN BUSINESS

$\mathcal{F}$irst of all, we can all agree that the Bible does not prohibit making money. The Apostle Paul worked as a tentmaker to provide for his personal needs (Acts 18:1-3; 2 Thess. 3:8). He taught the Thessalonians that if a man was unwilling to work, then he should be allowed to go hungry (2 Thess. 3:10). Without question the biblical emphasis is that a man should work diligently for the supply of his needs and the needs of his family.

Can we say, then, that a believer should make as much money as possible? No, such a statement would have to be qualified. He may make as much as possible, but with these reservations:

His work should not be allowed to take precedence over the things of the Lord. His paramount obligation is to seek first the kingdom of God and His righteousness (Mt. 6:33). Worship and service should not suffer because of the pressure of business.

His family obligations must not be neglected (1 Tim. 5:8). Ordinarily the more money a man makes, the less time he has for his wife and children. He cannot compensate for this by lavishing luxury and wealth on them;

this only adds to their spiritual and moral decay. They need the companionship and guidance of a godly husband and father far more than they need a bulging bank account.

His money should be made in a business that is reputable (Prov. 10:16). This should go without saying. It's questionable for a Christian to give his time to the production, distribution or advertising of commodities that endanger health or contribute to the lowering of morals. Neither should a Christian spend his life entertaining people who are on the highway to hell. Work should be constructive and for the common good.

Then too the believer should be sure that he is making his money honestly (Prov. 20:17). His business may be reputable enough but his methods may be crooked. For instance:

- falsifying income tax returns (Prov. 12:22).
- cheating on weights and measures (Prov. 11:1).
- bribing local inspectors (Prov. 17:23).
- advertising differences in products when no such differences exist (Prov. 20:6).
- fudging on expense accounts (Prov. 13:5).
- speculating in the market or on the stock exchange- just another form of gambling (Prov. 13:11).
- paying inadequate wages to employees (Prov. 22:16).

It is against this latter abuse that James cries out, *"Indeed the wages of the laborers who mowed your fields, which you kept back by fraud, cry out; and the cries of the reapers have reached the ears of the Lord of Sabaoth"* (Jas. 5:4).

The Christian may make as much money as he can without imperilling his own health. His body is the temple of the Holy Spirit (1 Cor. 6:19). He should not squander his health in the acquisition of wealth.

Finally, the Christian may make as much as he can without becoming covetous. He must never become a slave to mammon (Mt. 6:24). It is proper to make money but not to love it (Ps. 62:10).

To summarize, then, a Christian may earn as much as he can as long as he gives God first place, fulfills his family obligations, works constructively, deals honestly, guards his health, and avoids covetousness.

Sixteen

TO HAVE BUT NOT TO HOLD

*T*he next question we must face is this: "Is it wrong to hoard money?" As far as the New Testament is concerned, the answer is an emphatic Yes.

The Bible condemns no one for being rich. A person may receive an inheritance and become rich overnight. But it does have a lot to say about what we do with our riches.

Here is what the Bible teaches:

First of all, we are stewards of God (1 Cor. 4:1-2). That means that all we have belongs to Him, not to ourselves. Our responsibility is to use His money for His glory. The idea that 90% is for us to spend while the other 10% is the Lord's portion is a misconception of New Testament stewardship. It all belongs to the Lord.

The second point is that we are to be content with food and clothing. *"Having food and clothing, with these we shall be content"* (1 Tim. 6:8). Here the word for raiment means a covering or roofing. It can refer to any kind of shelter or clothing. So the verse says we should be satisfied with the necessities of life—food, clothing and housing. And in making allowance for roofing, the Lord here permits us to have more than He had when He was here; He had no place to lay His head (Mt. 8:20).

The Christian who owns a business will of course need fixed capital and working capital to carry on. He must be able to purchase raw materials, pay his employees, and meet the other financial demands that come to him day by day. Nothing in the Bible prohibits a Christian in business from having the funds necessary to operate.

Next, we should live as economically as possible, avoiding waste of every kind. After Jesus had fed the five thousand, He told the disciples to gather up the food that was left over (Jn. 6:12). His example teaches us to conserve wherever possible.

We buy so many unnecessary things. Especially at Christmas time, we spend a small fortune on worthless gifts that soon make their way to the attic or storeroom where they do no one any good.

We buy expensive things when cheaper items would often do just as well. (It is not always true that the cheaper item is the better buy. We must weigh price, quality, time saved, etc.).

We must discipline ourselves to resist the temptation to buy everything we want. And we must develop the habit of living frugally for the Son of Man's sake.

Everything above our necessities is to be put to work for the Lord (1 Tim. 6:8). Remember! It all belongs to Him. We are His stewards. Our business is to advance His cause on earth to the best of our ability.

It will immediately be objected that to plunge everything above food, clothing and housing into the work of

TO HAVE BUT NOT TO HOLD

the Lord is foolhardy, improvident, short-sighted.

Well, we have the record of one person who did it. She was a widow, and she cast her two mites into the treasury. Jesus did not reproach her. He said, *"Truly I say to you that this poor widow has put in more than all; for all these* [rich] *out of their abundance have put in offerings for God, but she out of her poverty put in all the livelihood that she had"* (Luke 21:3-4).

We are forbidden to lay up treasures on earth. The words of Scripture are plain and unmistakable:

> Do not lay up for yourselves treasures on earth, where moth and rust destroy and where thieves break in and steal; but lay up for yourselves treasures in heaven, where neither moth nor rust destroys and where thieves do not break in and steal. For where your treasure is, there your heart will be also (Mt. 6:19-21).

As far as most of us are concerned, these verses might just as well not be in the Bible. We believe Jesus spoke them. We believe they are divinely inspired. But we do not think that they apply to us. We do not obey them. And so as far as we are concerned, it is the same as if our Lord never spoke them.

Yet the truth remains that it is *sin* to lay up treasures on earth. It is directly contrary to the Word of God. What we call prudence and foresight is actually rebellion and iniquity. And it is still true that where our treasure is, there will our heart be also.

Dr. Samuel Johnson was once taken on a tour of a luxurious estate. He went through the mansion and over the well-kept grounds. Then he turned to his friends and said,

"These are the things that make it hard to die."

Finally we are to trust God for the future. God calls His people to a life of faith, to a life of dependence on Himself. He teaches us to pray, *"Give us this day our daily bread"* (Mt. 6:11). By the story of the manna, He teaches us to look to Him day by day for the supply of our needs (Ex. 16:14-22). He Himself is to be our security; we should not lean on the broken reeds of this world.

This, then, is our Lord's will for His people—that we should realize that we are stewards and that all we have belongs to Him; that we should be content with the necessities of life; that we should live as economically as possible; that we should put everything above our needs into the work of the Lord; that we should not lay up treasures on earth; and that we should trust Him for the future.

Seventeen

WHAT'S THE HARM IN IT?

*B*ut why is it wrong for a Christian to accumulate wealth, to hoard riches?

First of all, it's wrong because the Bible says so (Mt. 6:19); that should be sufficient reason. Why was it wrong for Adam and Eve to eat the fruit of the tree of the knowledge of good and evil? Because God said so. That should settle the matter for everyone of us.

But it is also wrong because it overlooks the vast spiritual need of the world today (Prov. 24:11-12). Millions of men and women, boys and girls have never heard the gospel of the grace of God. Millions do not have a Bible, or good gospel literature. Millions are dying without God, without Christ, without hope.

It is a form of spiritual fratricide to have the means of spreading the gospel and not to use them (Ezek. 33:6).

And it testifies loudly to a singular lack of God's love in the heart of the hoarder. For *"whoever has this world's goods, and sees his brother in need, and shuts up his heart from him, how does the love of God abide in him?"* (1 Jn. 3:17).

When two starving lepers in the Old Testament stumbled across a great supply of food, they satisfied their own hunger, then ran to share their find with others (2 Ki. 7:9). Should Christians under grace show less compassion than lepers under law?

Third, it's wrong to stockpile money because it is callous to the enormous physical needs of the world (Prov. 3:27-28; 11:26). The rich man in Luke 16 was quite unconcerned about the beggar at his gate. If he had just gone to his window and pulled aside the drape, he would have seen a genuine case of need, a worthy object on which to spend some of his money. But he didn't care.

The world is full of Lazaruses. They are lying at our gates. And Jesus is saying to us, *"You shall love your neighbor as yourself"* (Mt. 22:39). If we refuse to hear Him now, perhaps one day we will hear Him say to us,

> *I was hungry and you gave Me no food; I was thirsty and you gave Me no drink...Assuredly, I say to you, inasmuch as you did not do it to one of the least of these, you did not do it to Me* (Mt. 25:42, 45).

It is wrong for a Christian to lay up treasures on earth because it causes the enemies of God to blaspheme (Rom. 2:24). It provoked Voltaire to say, "When it comes to money, all men are of the same religion."

Many unsaved people are familiar with the teaching of Jesus. They know He taught that we should love our neighbor. They see the glaring inconsistency when those who profess to follow Jesus indulge in magnificent homes, luxurious cars, epicurean foods, and costly clothes.

It is time the Church woke up! Speak to educated

young people from all over the world—hear their criticisms of Christianity! They are not opposed to the ethics of Jesus, but they violently oppose the wealth of the Church and of Christians in a world of grinding poverty.

Someone once said that when the golden slippers climb the staircase, the hob-nailed boots are not far behind. Let the Church listen!

But we are not only concerned with the effect on unbelievers. We think of the effect on young Christians as well. They watch the example of their elders. More important than anything we can say is the way we live. Our sense of values is shown not so much by the stirring missionary message we give on Sunday, but by the goal we pursue on Monday through Friday.

Young people judge the reality of our pilgrimage by the assessed value of our "tent." They are not impressed by impassioned appeals for funds for the work of God by those who could meet the need with one stroke of the pen.

If our lives are spent in the accumulation of wealth, we must not be surprised if young people follow our example. And may we never forget the warning of the Lord Jesus:

> *It is impossible that no offenses should come, but woe to him through whom they do come! It would be better for him if a millstone were hung around his neck, and he were thrown into the sea, than that he should offend one of these little ones"* (Lk. 17:1-2).

Another reason why it is sinful to accumulate wealth is because it robs God (Mal. 3:8). We have already seen that all we have belongs to Him. If we can't use it directly in

113

the advancement of His interests, we should at least turn it over to those who can. To keep it laid up in a napkin is inexcusable (Lk. 19:20-26).

Failure to obey the Lord in the matter of financial stewardship closes portions of the Bible to us (Mt. 6:22-23). We become blind to passages that are quite simple on the face of them.

It is a strange twist of fallen nature but it is true.

> The further removed a study is from the personal center of our lives and responsibilities—as for example in physics and mathematics—the less will the sinful warpings of our nature affect our conclusion. The nearer a study brings us to our personal responsibility to our Creator the more does our sinful nature seek to blind our minds to truths which we do not want to believe and to encourage us to cling to some hypothesis which looks like it will relieve us of that responsibility.[1]

In that connection, Harrington C. Lees once wrote: "The most sensitive part of civilized man is his pocket, and one of the fiercest fights a preacher has to wage is when his preaching touches the pockets of his hearers."

Passages on self-denial have little seeming relevance when we are living at ease in Zion. And certainly we cannot effectively teach passages which we have not obeyed ourselves. So one of the curses of disobedience in this, as in all areas, is a mutilated Bible (Mt. 13:14-15).

The amassing of riches makes the life of faith practically impossible. Why? Because it is almost impossible to have riches and not trust in them. The man with money doesn't know how much he depends on it. *"The rich man's wealth is his strong city, and like a high wall in his own esteem"* (Prov. 18:11).

He depends on money to solve all his problems, to give him present enjoyment and future security. If he were to lose it all suddenly, his props and crutches would be gone and he would be in a state of panic.

The truth is that we would rather trust in a bank balance which we can see than a God whom we can't see. The thought of having no one or nothing but God to trust is sufficient to bring on a nervous collapse.

Left in His hands, we do not feel that we should be safe; whereas if we had our fortune in our own hands, and were secured against chances and changes by a few comfortable securities, we should feel safe enough. This feeling is, surely, very general: "We are all of us in danger of slipping into this form of unquiet distrust in the fatherly providence of God" (Samuel Cox).

God's will is that our lives should be a perpetual crisis of dependence on Him. We defeat His will in our lives when we lay up treasures on earth.

The life of faith is the only life that pleases God; without faith it is impossible to please Him (Heb. 11:6).

The life of faith is the only life that has true security. *"It is of faith...so that the promise might be sure"* (Rom. 4:16). Because nothing is as sure as the promise of God, it follows that the life of faith is the worry-free life. Nervous and emotional disorders arise from materialism, not from walking with God by faith.

The life of faith is the only life that gives all the glory

to God. When we walk by sight, we are glorifying human ingenuity and cleverness.

The life of faith speaks loudly to unbelievers and to other Christians. It testifies to all that there is a God in heaven who answers prayer. Faith is the opposite of sight; when you can see, you can't trust. To hoard wealth makes the life of faith impossible.

The life of faith does not follow automatically when a person becomes a Christian. It requires deliberate action on his part. This is especially true in an affluent society. The believer must put himself in a position where he is compelled to trust God. He can do this by selling all that he has and giving to the poor. It is only as he gets rid of his reserves and other false supports that he can truly launch out into the deep.

Not only so, it is dishonoring to our Lord to reign as kings in a world where He is still rejected and where His servants are being persecuted. Paul pictured the Corinthians as sitting in the most expensive seats at the stadium with crowns on their heads and wearing the finest of clothes. At the same time, he pictured the apostles in the arena, ready to be devoured by the wild beasts.

> *Oh, I know you are rich and flourishing! You've been living like kings, haven't you, while we've been away? I would to God that you were really kings in God's sight so that we might reign with you. I sometimes think that God means us, the messengers, to appear last in the procession of mankind, like the men who are to die in the arena. For indeed we are made a public spectacle before the angels of heaven and the eyes of men. We are looked upon as*

fools, for Christ's sake, but you are wise in the Christian faith. We are considered weak, but you have become strong: you have found honor, we little but contempt. Up to this very hour we are hungry and thirsty, ill-clad, knocked about and practically homeless. We still have to work for our living by manual labor. Men curse us, but we return a blessing: they make our lives miserable, but we take it patiently. They ruin our reputations, but we go on trying to win them for God. We are the world's rubbish, the scum of the earth, yes, up to this very day (1 Cor. 4:8-13, PHILLIPS).

The Corinthians were reigning as kings before Christ Himself was crowned. At coronation services, it is a mark of grave disrespect for lesser figures to put on their tiaras before the monarch is crowned.

To amass a fortune is directly contrary to the example of the Lord Jesus. He was infinitely rich, yet He voluntarily became poor in order to enrich us through His poverty (2 Cor. 8:9).

In the original language of the New Testament, there are two words which are translated poor. One word means the condition of a working man who has nothing beyond the essentials of life. The other means destitute or devoid of wealth. It is this second word that Paul uses to describe the Lord Jesus. How many of us are willing to follow Jesus all the way?

Another evil of riches is that they are detrimental to the prayer life. Where every material need is provided, why pray? More serious is the sham of asking God to do things when we can do them ourselves. For instance, how often do we as believers ask God to provide funds for certain projects when we ourselves could provide the money without delay. Oftentimes the Lord's own money is not available to Him.

Finally, it is wrong for Christians to accumulate wealth because it might encourage others to become Christians with the hope of becoming rich. The poverty of the early believers was an asset, not a liability.

> A religion which turned the world upside-down, while its first preachers were all poor men, must needs have been from heaven. If the apostles had possessed money to give their hearers, or been followed by armies to frighten them, an infidel might well deny that there was anything wonderful in their success. But the poverty of our Lord's disciples cut away such arguments from beneath the infidel's feet. With a doctrine most unpalatable to the natural heart, with nothing whatever to bribe or compel obedience—a few lowly Galileans shook the world, and changed the face of the Roman empire. Only one thing can account for this. The gospel of Christ, which these men proclaimed, was the truth of God.[3]

Gilmour of Mongolia wrote: "If I go among them rich, they will be continually begging and perhaps regard me more as a source of gifts than anything else. If I go with nothing but the gospel, there will be nothing to distract their attention from the unspeakable gift."

Peter and John met a lame beggar at the gate of the temple. When he asked them for a handout, Peter said, *"Silver and gold I do not have, but what I do have I give you: In the name of Jesus Christ of Nazareth, rise up and walk"* (Acts 3:6).

Perhaps some will say that preachers should be poor, but not necessarily all Christians. But where does the Bible teach a different economic standard for preachers and for others, for missionaries and for folks at home?

Eighteen

THE CASE FOR FROZEN ASSETS

$\mathcal{S}$o much then for the reasons why it is wrong for a Christian to hoard wealth. Now we must turn to the arguments which are commonly used to justify believers who have saved money to provide for their future and the future of their families.

The first argument runs something like this: It is only reasonable that we should set aside money for our old age. What is going to happen to us when we are no longer able to work? We should always anticipate the rainy day. God expects us to use common sense.

This reasoning sounds convincing but it is not the language of faith. Reserves are crutches and props which become a substitute for trust in the Lord. We can't trust when we can see.

Once we decide to provide for our future, we run into these problems. How much will be enough? How long will we live? Will there be a depression? Will there be inflation? Will we have heavy medical bills?

It is impossible to know how much will be enough. Therefore we spend our lives amassing wealth to provide for a few short years of retirement. In the meantime, God has been robbed and our own life has been spent in seeking security where it cannot be found.

How much better it is to work diligently for our current necessities, serve the Lord to the maximum extent, put everything above present needs into the work of the Lord, and trust Him for the future. To those who put Him first, He has promised, *"all these things shall be added to you"* (Mt. 6:33).

And to the Philippians who were using the Lord's money for the spread of the truth, Paul wrote: *"My God shall supply all your need according to His riches in glory by Christ Jesus"* (Phil. 4:19).

There is unspeakable tragedy in the current philosophy of giving one's life to the acquisition of wealth with the hope of giving one's retirement to the Lord. It means giving the best of our life to a corporation, then giving the fag-end to Jesus. Even then, the fag-end is so uncertain. Often it is finished before we get the Bible dusted off.

It seems like common sense to provide for a rainy day. But the truth of the matter was well stated by Cameron Thompson: "God pours out His choicest blessings on those who are anxious that nothing shall stick to their hands. Individuals who value the rainy day above the present agony of the world will get no blessing from God."

A second argument used to justify laying up treasures on earth is based on 1 Timothy 5:8, *"But if anyone does not provide for his own, and especially for those of his household, he has denied the faith and is worse than an unbeliever."*

In this passage, Paul is dealing with the care of widows

in the church. He states that the Christian relatives of a widow are responsible to care for her. If she has no relatives to do this, then the church should care for her.

But the important thing to see is that Paul isn't speaking about laying aside funds to support the widow sometime in the future. Rather he is speaking of her current needs. Christians should take care of destitute relatives day by day; if they don't, this is a practical denial of the Christian faith which teaches love and generosity, Even unbelievers look after their own people. A believer who doesn't is therefore worse than unbelievers.

The verse says nothing about reserves, endowments, or investment portfolios. It deals with current necessities, not future obligations.

The third argument is closely related to the second. Many Christian parents feel that it is part of their responsibility to leave a sizeable inheritance to their children. They feel that that is part of what is meant by providing for one's own (1 Tim. 5:8). It doesn't make any difference whether the children are believers or not; the deep desire is there to leave them a respectable nest-egg.

Second Corinthians 12:14 is sometimes used to teach that parents should save money so that they can leave it to their children. The passage reads: *"...For the children ought not to lay up for the parents, but the parents for the children."*

As stated previously, the immediate context is dealing with the subject of Paul's financial support. He had not taken any money from the Corinthians, but had been supported by gifts from other churches while he was preaching at Corinth (2 Cor. 11:7-8). Now he was ready to go back to Corinth again, but he assured them that he would not be burdensome to them (12:14), that is, he would not depend on any financial assistance from them. He was not interested in their material possessions but in their spiritual welfare.

It is at this point he adds, *"...For the children ought not to lay up for the parents, but the parents for the children."* The Corinthians were the children and Paul was the parent (1 Cor. 4:15). He was saying to them—obviously in irony—that they should not support him; rather he should support them. He said it in irony, because they actually should have contributed to his support (1 Cor. 9:11, 14), but he had chosen to forego this right in their case.

The important thing to see is that this passage has nothing to do with storing up reserves for the future. That was not the issue at all. It was a matter of current needs, and Paul was saying, "After all—children don't generally support their parents; it's the parents who provide for the children."

Certainly the practice of building up an inheritance for one's children finds no support in the New Testament. The greatest legacy which parents can leave is a spiritual one, but preoccupation with making money is the very thing that hinders the provision of this inheritance.

And think of the evils that have arisen from the financial legacies that Christians have left.

Many young people have been ruined spiritually by having wealth suddenly thrust upon them. They have become intoxicated with materialism and pleasure, and spoiled for the service of Christ.

Then think of the conflicts that have arisen in otherwise peaceful families as a result of wills and estates. Sister has become jealous of sister, and brother of brother. Bitter quarrels have continued throughout the rest of life.

A family quarrel over an inheritance is recorded in Luke 12:13-14. Jesus refused to become involved in it; He hadn't come to earth for that kind of work. But He took time to issue a stern warning against covetousness to the unhappy man who wasn't named in the will.

Then we have this situation: Parents work hard all their lives to be able to leave something to the children. Later they become aged and infirm, a care to their family, and the ungrateful children can hardly wait for their parents to die in order to get their hands on the money.

Money left to unsaved children or to a Christian son or daughter married to an unbeliever has often made its way to a false church and has been used for the suppression of the gospel rather than for its propagation. Think of it! The money of believers used to fight the Truth!

And then we must think of the enormous amounts of money that go to the government in inheritance taxes, and to lawyers for legal fees. All this could have been used in the salvation of souls.

Some Christians try to avoid some of these griefs by leaving their money to Christian organizations. But there is no guarantee that the money will ever get to those organizations. Wills are constantly being contested and broken. And even apart from that, the practice of leaving your money lacks scriptural support. There is no assurance that the organizations will still be true to the Lord and His Word by the time the will is probated.

Believers will not be rewarded for what they leave in a will. The minute they die, the money ceases to be theirs; it becomes the property of their estate.

Men heap up riches and do not know who will gather them (Ps. 39:6). The only way to be sure that your money is used for the Lord is to give while you live. And this is the only way to obtain a future reward.

We say we believe in the imminent return of the Lord Jesus. Then we should realize that the nearer we approach His coming, the less value our material possessions have. When He does come, our wealth will have no value for us or for the work of God. So the best thing is to put our possessions to work for Jesus *now*.

Then this argument arises: "If everyone put everything above a modest living into the work of the Lord, how would we live? Someone must stand by the stuff."

How would we live? The answer is, "More by faith and less by sight!" There is no use arguing that it wouldn't work because it did work in the early days of the Church.

All who believed were together, and had all things in common, and sold their possessions and goods, and divided them among all, as anyone had need (Acts 2:44-45).

"Nor was there anyone among them who lacked; for all who were possessors of lands or houses sold them, and brought the proceeds of the things that were sold, and laid them at the apostles' feet; and they distributed to each as anyone had need" (Acts 4:34-35).

In writing to the Corinthians, Paul taught that our material possessions should be fluid, not frozen. Whenever we are aware of a genuine need, our funds should flow to meet that need. Then if we ourselves are ever in need, funds would likewise flow to us. In this way, there would be a constant equalizing among God's people.

For I do not mean that others should be eased and you burdened; but by an equality, that now at this time your abundance may supply their lack, that their abundance also may supply your lack— that there may be equality. As it is written, "He who gathered much had nothing left over, and he who gathered little had no lack." (2 Cor. 8:13-15).

In other words, if any person has really lived devotedly for the Lord and has been faithful in the stewardship of his possessions, other believers should be willing and happy to share with him if the need ever arises.

If we are honest with ourselves, we have to admit that the thought of being dependent on others is repugnant to us. We are proud of our independence. But is this not a manifestation of the self-life and not of the life of the Lord Jesus in us?

Paul's instructions for the care of widows in 1 Timothy 5:3-13 presupposes a church where the love of God is shed abroad in human hearts, where the saints exercise mutual care for one another, and where money flows freely wherever true needs exist. And if it be contended that though it worked in the early days of the Church, it wouldn't work today, the answer is simply this: it is working today. There are Christians who are living this life of

127

faith. And there is a power and attractiveness about their lives that cannot be denied.

But someone will object, "Didn't Paul say, *'I know how to be abased, and I know how to abound'*" (Phil. 4:12)? The questioner obviously pictures the abased Paul wandering across a trackless desert, hungry, thirsty, weary, ill-clothed and ill-shod. But then the abounding Paul is seen as a bronzed young man climbing out of his convertible chariot at some seaside resort, clothed in the latest fashions from Palm Springs, and luxuriating for two weeks on the American plan. In other words, he could rough it or he could live high.

But that is not exactly what Paul is saying in the letter to Philippi. We must remember that that letter was written from prison, not from a seaside resort. And writing from prison, he said, *"I have all and abound. I am full, having received from Epaphroditus the things sent from you, a sweet-smelling aroma, an acceptable sacrifice, well pleasing to God"* (Phil. 4:18).

We would think that imprisonment would be on the *abased* side of the ledger, but Paul put it on the *abounding* side. Therefore, it is not right for us to use Philippians 4:12 to justify lives of wealth and luxury. That is not what the verse teaches.

Well, then what about the verse that says that God has given us richly all things to enjoy? (1 Tim. 6:17). This is quoted often as scriptural proof that the believer should enjoy "the good things of life" which means that it is all right for him to indulge in the latest and the best. His slogan is, "Nothing too good for the people of God."

But he forgets the context once again. Notice how the verse begins: *"Command those who are rich in this present age not to be haughty, nor to trust in uncertain riches..."* (1 Tim. 6:17). In other words, far from being an excuse for self-indulgence, the words are found in a passage which sounds a solemn charge to the rich.

Well, what does it mean, that God has given us richly all things to enjoy? It means that He has not given us these things to hoard; He wants us to *enjoy* them by sharing them with others. This is clear from the two verses that follow:

> *Let them do good, that they be rich in good works, ready to give, willing to share, storing up for themselves a good foundation for the time to come, that they may lay hold on eternal life* (1 Tim. 6:18-19).

Enjoyment of riches is not found in possessing them but in using them for the glory of God and for the good of others.

Then we are often reminded that Abraham was a rich man (Gen. 13:2), and yet he was called a friend of God (Jas. 2:23). This is, of course, true, but we must remember that Abraham lived in the Old Testament period where material prosperity was promised to those who obeyed the Lord. Riches were a sign of God's blessing. Is this true in the dispensation of the grace of God? It would be more accurate to say that adversity is the blessing of this period.

In the parable of Lazarus and the rich man (Lk. 16:19-31), Old Testament standards were reversed. The rich

129

man was condemned because he failed to use his wealth for others but hoarded it for himself.

But then are we not taught to learn from the ant?

Go to the ant, you sluggard! Consider her ways and be wise, which, having no captain, overseer or ruler, provides her supplies in the summer, and gathers her food in the harvest" (Prov. 6:6-8).

Does this not show that the ant makes provision for its future, and are we not told to imitate it in this respect? Yes, but the important thing to remember is that while the ant's future is on this earth, the Christian's future is in heaven. The believer is a pilgrim and a stranger here; his home is above. And he should be laying up treasure for his future.

But as far as his life here is concerned, he is forbidden to take anxious thought for tomorrow—what he will eat or what he will wear (Mt. 6:25). Rather he is told to imitate the birds, which never build storage barns next to their nests; yet our heavenly Father feeds them. And the argument is that if God cares for sparrows, how much more does He care for us!

A final argument is that someone must be rich to reach the rich. The Christians in the first years of the Church did not realize this.

History relates that the early Christians, many of them, were so eager to carry Christ's gospel everywhere that they even hired themselves out as servants or sold themselves as slaves, that they might be admitted into the homes of the rich and great among the heathen, to live there, and thus have opportunity to tell in those homes of the love of Jesus and His salvation.[1]

Nineteen

WHAT DOES THE BIBLE SAY?

*N*ow we have discussed the principal arguments that are used to justify Christians living in riches in a world where demoralizing poverty prevails. In striking contrast to these few weak arguments are the many portions of the Word which warn us of the perils of riches.

> *A faithful man will abound with blessings, but he who hastens to be rich will not go unpunished...A man with an evil eye hastens after riches, and does not consider that poverty will come upon him* (Prov. 28:20, 22).

The frantic quest for material riches is a pursuit unworthy of one who was created in the image and after the likeness of God.

> *No one can serve two masters; for either he will hate the one and love the other, or else he will be loyal to the one and despise the other. You cannot serve God and mammon* (Mt. 6:24).

God and money are here presented as two masters whose interests are so opposed that it is impossible to serve both. This strikes a death-blow at the desire to live for two worlds, to be rich now and be rich then, to enjoy wealth below and be rewarded for it above. Jesus said you can't have both; you must choose one or the other.

> *Then Jesus said to His disciples, "Assuredly, I say to you that it is hard for a rich man to enter the kingdom of heaven. And again I say to you, it is easier for a camel to go through the eye of a needle than for a rich man to enter the kingdom of God."*
>
> *When His disciples heard it, they were greatly astonished, saying, "Who then can be saved?" But Jesus looked at them and said to them, "With men this is impossible, but with God all things are possible"* (Mt. 19:23-26).

I wonder if we consider these words of Jesus seriously enough. He did not say it was difficult for a rich man to enter into the kingdom of God; He said it was humanly impossible. Some explain the needle's eye as a smaller door in the city gate. A camel had to stoop low to get through it. But the needle spoken of here is a sewing needle, and no camel can get through its eye. Only a special miracle of divine power can enable a rich man to enter the kingdom. Why then do we strive so hard to defend that which is such a hindrance to man's eternal welfare?

"But woe to you who are rich, for you have received your consolation" (Lk. 6:24). Here the holy Son of God pronounced a woe upon rich people. The word can only be taken literally here. It cannot mean anything but rich. Why then do we seek to bless whom God has not blessed?

> *Sell what you have and give alms; provide yourselves money bags which do not grow old, a treasure in the heavens that does not fail, where no thief approaches nor moth destroys. For where your treasure is, there your heart will be also* (Lk. 12:33-34).

WHAT DOES THE BIBLE SAY?

These words were spoken to the disciples (see v. 22). We try to avoid them by saying that they were not intended for us. But why not? In resisting such verses, we are only resisting a blessing.

How utterly in keeping with this age of grace it is for us to sell our prized possessions—our diamonds and other jewelry, our original paintings, our antique furniture, our sterling silver, our stamp collections—and put the proceeds to work in the salvation of souls throughout the world. Where is our heart? Is it in the vault of the local bank? Or is it in heaven? *"Where your treasure is, there your heart will be also."*

> *So when Jesus heard these things, He said to him, "You still lack one thing. Sell all that you have and distribute to the poor, and you will have treasure in heaven; and come, follow Me." But when he heard this, he became very sorrowful, for he was very rich* (Lk. 18:22-23).

We are constantly told that the rich young ruler was a special case, that by no stretch of the imagination was the command to sell all intended for everyone. Even if that were so, the teaching is not substantially different from what is found in the passage we have just considered (Lk. 12:33-34).

> *Now godliness with contentment is great gain. For we brought nothing into this world, and it is certain we can carry nothing out. And having food and clothing, with these we shall be content. But those who desire to be rich fall into temptation and a snare, and into many foolish and harmful lusts which drown men in destruc-*

tion and perdition. For the love of money is a root of all kinds of evil, for which some have strayed from the faith in their greediness, and pierced themselves through with many sorrows. But you, O man of God, flee these things and pursue righteousness, godliness, faith, love, patience, gentleness (1 Tim. 6:6-11).

Paul warned that those who covet money pierce themselves through with many sorrows. What are the sorrows that he referred to?

First is the worry that invariably accompanies wealth. *"The abundance of the rich will not permit him to sleep"* (Eccl. 5:12). The riches that are supposed to bring security actually bring the opposite—constant fear of theft, inflation, or declines in the stock market.

Second is the sorrow of seeing one's children ruined spiritually by an over-abundance of material things. Few children of wealthy Christian parents are going on for the Lord.

Then there is the bitterness of having riches fail you when you need them most.

The rich person never knows how many friends he has. This may seem to be contradicted by Proverbs 14:20 which says, *"The poor man is hated even by his own neighbor, but the rich has many friends."* But are they true friends—or are they just playing the part for selfish reasons?

Riches inevitably fail to satisfy the heart, but create an incessant craving for more (Eccl. 2:8, 4:8; 5:10).

Finally, wealth often has adverse effects on a person's character, producing pride (Prov. 28:11) and rough man-

ners (Prov. 18:23; Jas. 2:5-7), for example.
Matthew Henry reminds us:

> The Hebrew word for riches signifies 'heavy'; and riches are a burden—a burden of care in getting them, a burden of fear in keeping them, a burden of temptation, a burden of sorrow, and a burden accounting for them at last."

> *Command those who are rich in this present age not to be haughty, nor to trust in uncertain riches but in the living God, who gives us richly all things to enjoy. Let them do good, that they be rich in good works, ready to give, willing to share, storing up for themselves a good foundation for the time to come, that they may lay hold on eternal life* (1 Tim. 6:17-19).

In these verses, we are told to *"Command those who are rich..."* Yet how many servants of God fulfill this commission? How many of us have ever charged the rich? Most of us have never even heard a message on this verse. Yet there probably was never a time when this revolutionary message was more needed.

In order to preach the message, we must first of all be obedient to it ourselves. If we are living by sight instead of by faith, we cannot tell others not to lay up treasures on earth. The life seals the lips.

God is looking for men of the prophetic breed who will fearlessly speak His word in spite of consequences. Men like Amos who cried out:

> *Hear this word, you cows of Bashan, who are on the mountain of Samaria, who oppress the poor, who crush the needy, who say to your husbands, "Bring wine, let us drink!" The Lord God has*

sworn by His holiness: "Behold, the days shall come upon you when He will take you away with fishhooks, and your posterity with fishhooks. You will go out through broken walls, each one straight ahead of her, and you will be cast into Harmon," says the Lord (Amos 4:1-3).

Or men like Haggai who thundered: *"Is it time for you yourselves to dwell in your paneled houses, and this temple to lie in ruins?"* (Hag. 1:4).

Of course, the prophets were never popular. Their presence was an embarrassment to their contemporaries. They were pressurized financially and ostracized socially. At times they were persecuted, and if nothing else would silence them, they were killed. It didn't matter; they would rather speak the truth than live a lie.

Materialism and wealth are hindering the flow of spiritual power in the Church today. Revival will never come while believers are reigning as kings. Who will arise and call God's people back to lives of faith and of sacrifice?

Who will show people how to lay hold on life that is life indeed (1 Tim. 6:19)? C. H. Mackintosh wrote, "The only real life is to live in the light of eternity—to use all we possess for the promotion of God's glory and with an eye to the everlasting mansions. This, and only this is life in earnest."

Let...the rich [glory] in his humiliation, because as a flower of the field he will pass away. For no sooner has the sun risen with a burning heat than it withers the grass; its flower falls, and its beautiful appearance perishes. So the rich man also will fade away in his pursuits (Jas. 1:10-11).

The rich man is not told to rejoice in his riches, but in anything that brings him low. Why is this? Because riches are perishable as the grass, whereas spiritual experiences and lessons are of eternal value.

> *Come now, you rich, weep and howl for your miseries that are coming upon you! Your riches are corrupted, and your garments are moth-eaten. Your gold and silver are corroded, and their corrosion will be a witness against you and will eat your flesh like fire. You have heaped up treasure in the last days. Indeed the wages of the laborers who mowed your fields, which you kept back by fraud, cry out; and the cries of the reapers have reached the ears of the Lord of Sabaoth. You have lived on the earth in pleasure and luxury; you have fattened your hearts as in a day of slaughter. You have condemned, you have murdered the just; he does not resist you* (Jas. 5:1-6).

Here the Spirit of God cries out against the hoarding of wealth (v. 3), against making money by failure to pay fair wages (v. 4), against luxurious living (v. 5), and against taking advantage of innocent people who are helpless to resist (v. 6). It is needless to argue whether these verses were written to believers or unbelievers. If the shoe fits, we should put it on!

> *Because you say, "I am rich, have become wealthy, and have need of nothing" and do not know that you are wretched, miserable, poor, blind, and naked—"I counsel you to buy from Me gold refined in the fire, that you may be rich; and white garments, that you may be clothed, that the shame of your nakedness may not be revealed; and anoint your eyes with eye salve, that you may see.*

"As many as I love, I rebuke and chasten. Therefore be zealous and repent" (Rev. 3:17-19).

This is the Lord's closing message to the churches, His cutting words to the church of the Laodiceans. They really don't need exposition. We know what they mean. And we know that they have a particular application to ourselves. All they need is our obedience.

A Warning to the Lazy!

There is always a danger that a chapter like this might be used as an excuse for indolence. Someone with a decided aversion for work might read it and say, "That is what I've always believed."

Well, this message is not for the shiftless or for those who feel the world (or the church) owes them a living. God has a different message for people like that: "Get out of bed and go to work" (see 2 Thess. 3:6-12).

This message is for people who are serious, industrious, hard working. Those who diligently provide for the present needs of their families, and who live first and foremost for the interests of the Lord Jesus can trust God for the future.

A Warning Against Judging!

There is another danger to be avoided. It is the danger of condemning individuals because of their material possessions. We must not judge others, or question their devotedness to the Lord.

It is one thing to declare the principles of the Word of

God on the subject of riches. It is quite another thing to go through a Christian's home, take a quick mental inventory of his net worth, then wave an accusing finger at him. We are all responsible to hear what God says, then to make the application in our own lives. The current needs of a large family will obviously be greater than those of a single person.

We cannot tell anyone else what it is going to mean for him to be obedient to the Lord's commands. As stewards, each of us must give account to God for ourselves, not for others. So may the Lord deliver us from a harsh, critical, censorious spirit toward other individuals!

CONCLUSION

It seems clear from the Word of God that believers should be satisfied with food, clothing and housing; that they should be industrious in providing these current needs for their families; and that everything in excess should go into the work of God. They should not try to provide for their own future security, but should trust the Lord for this. The great aim of their life should be to serve the Lord Jesus Christ; everything else should be subordinated to this.

This is the life that is taught in the Gospels, practiced in the Acts, and expounded in the Epistles. The prime example is the Lord Jesus Himself. But the question may arise, "How can I make this practical in my own life? What should I do?"

The first thing is to give ourselves to the Lord (2 Cor. 8:5). When He has us, it is sure He has our possessions.

Then as the Lord puts His finger on various areas of our lives, we should respond immediately. Perhaps He will create an uneasiness in our hearts about eating in expensive restaurants? Or about spending money on expensive sports equipment? As we look at that late-model, high priced car or motorcycle, He may show us the possibility of getting a more modest vehicle and putting the difference into the spread of the gospel. He might revolutionize our clothes closet, in order to clothe many with God's robe of righteousness. A change to less-demanding employment might be indicated. We might lose our love for that expensive home and think of moving to less pretentious quarters.

When God begins to speak to us about these matters, we will know. It will be so clear that to refuse will be positive disobedience.

The third thing is this: *"Whatever He says to you, do it"* (Jn. 2:5). Friends may misunderstand you. Relatives may reproach you. There will be repercussions. Only follow Jesus, and leave the consequences to Him.

Put everything above current needs to work for God. Pray for guidance. Ask Him to show you where you should send it. He will! May the Lord permit us to see in our lives and in our generation a return to this kind of Christian devotedness. As John Wesley once prayed:

Oh that God would give me the thing which I long for! That before I go hence and am no more seen, I may see a people wholly devoted to God, crucified to the world, and the world crucified to them. A people truly given up to God in body, soul and substance! How cheerfully would I then say, "Now lettest Thou Thy servant depart in peace."

LORD, BREAK ME!

The final chapters were originally published as a separate booklet with the same name. It would be a mistake to undertake any discussion of discipleship without emphasizing this crucial subject.

Twenty

GOD VALUES BROKEN THINGS

"The brokenness of spirit which makes no resistance to the Father's hand is a main element of fertility in souls wherein He works. It is not power He seeks from us, but weakness; not resistant force, but 'yieldingness' to Him. All power is His: His strength is perfected in weakness" (Author Unknown).

Thirty years after Andrew Murray wrote *Abide in Christ,* he said: "I would like you to know that a minister or Christian author may often be led to say more than he has experienced. I had not then [when he wrote *Abide in Christ*] experienced all that I wrote of. I cannot say that I have experienced it all perfectly now."

Was it not in this same spirit that the Apostle Paul wrote, *"Not that I have already attained, or am already perfected; but I press on, that I may lay hold of that for which Christ Jesus has also laid hold of me"* (Phil. 3:12).

I share the same sentiment with regard to the following chapter, "Lord, Break Me!" The burden of the Lord is on me to write these things. The truth is too sublime and too urgent to be withheld simply because I have failed to experience it in full. To whatever extent I have failed, I make the things I have written the aspiration of my heart.

Twenty-One

GOD WANTS US ALL TO BE BROKEN

*U*sually when something is broken, its value declines or disappears altogether. Broken dishes, broken bottles, broken mirrors are generally scrapped. Even a crack in furniture or a tear in cloth greatly reduces its resale value.

But it isn't that way in the spiritual realm. God puts a premium on broken things—especially on broken people. That is why we read such verses as: *"The Lord is near to those who have a broken heart, and saves such as have a contrite spirit"* (Ps. 34:18). *"The sacrifices of God are a broken spirit, a broken and a contrite heart—these, O God, You will not despise"* (Ps. 51:17). God knows how to resist the proud and haughty, but He cannot resist a person who is humble and contrite. God opposes the proud, but gives grace to the humble (Jas. 4:6). There is something in our brokenness that appeals to His compassion and power. And so part of His wonderful purpose for our lives is that we should be broken—broken in heart, broken in spirit, and broken even in body (2 Cor. 4:6-18).

CONVERSION: A FORM OF BROKENNESS

We are introduced to the breaking process prior to our conversion when the Holy Spirit begins His work of convicting us of sin. He must get us to the place where we are willing to confess we are lost, unworthy, deserving only of hell. We fight every step of the way. But He continues to wrestle with us until our pride is shattered, our boasting tongue is silenced, and all resistance gone. Lying at the foot of the Cross, we finally whisper, "Lord Jesus, save me!" The shrew has been tamed, the sinner has been mastered, the colt has been broken.

Yes, the colt has been broken. By nature the colt is a wild, lawless creature. At the merest suggestion of a bridle or a saddle, it will rear, bolt, leap, and kick. It may be a beautiful, well-proportioned animal, but as long as it is unbroken, it is useless as far as service is concerned. But then comes the painful, prolonged process of bending the colt's will so that it will submit to the harness. Once the colt's will has been conquered by a higher will, the animal finds the real reason for its existence.

In this connection, it is good for us to remember that the Lord Jesus was a carpenter in Nazareth, and as such He may have made wooden yokes. Someone has beautifully suggested that if there had been a sign over the door of His shop, it probably would have read, "My yokes fit well." But the point for us is that our divine Lord is still a yoke maker. He says, *"Take My yoke upon you and learn from Me, for I am gentle and lowly in heart, and you will find rest for your souls. For My yoke is easy and My burden is light"* (Mt. 11:29-30).

However, yokes are only for those who are broken and submissive. Our wills must be subdued and yielded before we can learn of Him. He was gentle and lowly in

heart. We must become like Him, and only in so doing
will we find rest for our hearts.

ELEMENTS OF BROKENNESS

But that brings us to the basic question, "What is
meant by true brokenness? How does it manifest itself in
a believer's life? What are some of its basic elements?"

Repentance, confession, apology: Perhaps one of the
first things we think of is a readiness to confess sin to
God and to those we have wronged. The broken man is
quick to repent. He does not try to sweep sin under the
carpet. He does not try to forget it with the excuse, "Time
heals all things." He rushes into the presence of God and
cries, "I have sinned." Then he goes to whoever has been
hurt by his actions and says, "I was wrong. I am sorry. I
want you to forgive me." If on the one hand he knows the
scalding shame of having to apologize, on the other he
knows the great release of having a clear conscience and
of walking in the light.

True confession does not gloss over sin or blunt its
reality. It is not like the unbroken matron who said with
hauteur, "If I have done anything wrong, I am willing to
be forgiven." Genuine repentance says, "I have done
wrong and I'm here to say that I'm sorry."

David's life was clouded by sin and failure, but the
thing that endeared him to God's heart was his deep pen-
itence. In Psalms 32 and 51 we retrace with him his trans-
gressions, sin, and iniquity. We watch him during the time
when he refused to repent; life then was physical, mental,

and spiritual misery. Nothing went right. It seemed that everything was out of joint. Finally he broke. He confessed and God forgave. Then the bells began to ring again and David recovered his song.

In the New Testament, Paul gives us an illustration of brokenness. It was at the time he appeared before the chief priests and Sanhedrin in Jerusalem. When he prefaced his remarks with a statement that he had always lived in good conscience, the high priest was infuriated and ordered that the prisoner be slapped on the mouth.

The apostle snapped back, *"God will strike you, you whitewashed wall! For you sit to judge me according to the law, and do you command me to be struck contrary to the law?"* (Acts 23:3).

The attendants were shocked by Paul's scathing rebuke. Didn't he know that he was speaking to the high priest? Actually the apostle did not know. Maybe Ananias was not wearing his official robes or occupying his usual seat. Or perhaps it was Paul's weak eyesight again. Whatever the reason, he had not intentionally spoken evil of the duly constituted ruler. So he quickly apologized for his words, quoting Exodus 22:28, *"You shall not revile God, nor curse a ruler of your people."* The apostle had a low breaking point. He demonstrated his spiritual maturity by his readiness to say, "I was wrong. I am sorry."

Restitution. Closely connected with this first aspect of brokenness is prompt restitution, wherever it is called for. If I have stolen, damaged, or injured something, or if someone else has suffered loss because of my misbehavior, it is not enough to apologize. Justice demands that the loss be repaid. This applies to what happened before my conversion as well as to what happens afterwards.

After Zacchaeus had received the Lord Jesus, he remembered some of the crooked deals he had pulled as a tax-collector. It was a divine instinct that taught him immediately that these wrongs must be made right. So he said to the Lord, *"...if I have taken anything from anyone by false accusation, I restore fourfold"* (Lk. 19:7-9). Here the "if" does not express any doubt or indecision. The idea is "in every case where I have defrauded anyone of anything, I restore it fourfold." His determination to make restitution was a fruit of his conversion. The "fourfold" was a gauge of the vitality of his new life.

There are cases where it is impossible to make restitution. Perhaps records have been destroyed, or exact amounts have been forgotten with the passing of time. God knows all about this. All He wants is that we pay back what we owe in every case where we can.

And this should always be done in the Name of the Lord Jesus. There is no glory for God in it if I just say, "I stole this. I am sorry. Now I want to pay you back." The action should be linked with a testimony for Christ, such as, "I have recently become a Christian through faith in the Lord Jesus Christ. The Lord has been speaking to me about some tools I stole from you five years ago. I have come to apologize and to return the tools." Every act of righteousness or kindness which a Christian does should be combined with a witness for the Savior so that He and not self gets the glory.

A forgiving spirit. A third element of brokenness is the willingness to forgive when we have been wronged. In many cases this takes as much grace as apologizing or making restitution. Actually the New Testament is surprisingly explicit in laying down instructions for us in this manner of forgiving others.

First of all, whenever we have been wronged, we should immediately forgive the person in our hearts (Eph. 4:32). We do not go to him yet and tell him he is forgiven, but in our hearts we have actually forgiven him.

> The moment a man wrongs me, I must forgive him. Then my soul is free. If I hold the wrong against him, I sin against God, and against him and jeopardize my forgiveness with God. Whether the man repents, makes amends, asks my pardon or not, makes no difference. I have instantly forgiven him. He must face God with the wrong he has done, but that is his affair and God's and not mine, save that I should help him according to Matthew 18:15, etc. But whether this succeeds or not and before this even begins, I must forgive him.[1]

There are multitudes of little wrongs that can be forgiven and forgotten immediately. It is real victory when we can do it. *"Love...does not keep account of evil or gloat over the wickedness of other people"* (1 Cor. 13:7, Phillips). Clara Barton, founder of the American Red Cross, was once asked, "Don't you remember the mean thing that that woman said to you?" Her reply was, "I not only don't remember; I distinctly remember forgetting."

If the wrong is of a more serious nature and you do not feel it would be righteous to let it pass, then the next step

152

is to go to the offender and speak to him about it (Mt. 18:15). If he repents, then you must forgive him. *"And if he sins against you seven times in a day, and seven times in a day returns to you, saying, 'I repent,' you shall forgive him"* (Lk. 17:4). It is only right that we should be willing to forgive indefinitely. After all, we have been and are forgiven times without number.

Notice that you are not to go and tell everyone else about the offender's fault (what we almost invariably do). *"Go and tell him his fault, between you and him alone."* The obvious strategy is to keep these differences as confined as possible.

As soon as the offending brother confesses, you tell him he is forgiven. You have already forgiven him in your heart, but now you can administer forgiveness to him.

But suppose he refuses to repent. Then in accordance with Matthew 18:16, you *"take with you one or two more, that by the mouth of two or three witnesses every word may be established."*

If he refuses to listen to the two or three witnesses, then the matter should be taken to the local fellowship of Christians. The purpose in all this is not vindictiveness or punishment, but the restoration of the offending brother.

If this final effort fails, he is to be looked upon as a Gentile and a tax-collector. In other words, you no longer treat him as one who is in fellowship in the local church. Since he is not acting like a Christian, you accept him on his own ground. You count him as an unbeliever. But as soon as he repents, then you forgive him and full fellowship is restored.

God hates an unforgiving spirit, the determination to carry grudges to the grave, the unwillingness to let bygones be bygones. This is brought out forcefully in the parable of the debtor servant (Mt. 18:23-35). When he himself was bankrupt, he had been forgiven by the king a million dollars. But then he was unwilling to forgive a fellow servant a few dollars. The lesson is clear. Since God forgave us when we were in debt over our heads, we should be willing to forgive others who owe us trifles.

Enduring wrong without retaliating. But there are other aspects of brokenness. One is the humble spirit that suffers for doing right and does not retaliate. Here, of course, our Lord is the prime example, *"who, when He was reviled, did not revile in return; when He suffered, He did not threaten, but committed Himself to Him who judges righteously"* (1 Pet. 2:23). We have all been called to this type of life.

> *For this is commendable, if because of conscience toward God one endures grief, suffering wrongfully. For what credit is it if, when you are beaten for your faults, you take it patiently? But when you do good and suffer, if you take it patiently, this is commendable before God* (1 Pet. 2:19-20).

In his book, *From Grace to Glory,* Murdoch Campbell reminds us that John Wesley had a wife who made his life a trial of fire. For hours she would literally drag him around the room by his hair. And the founder of Methodism never uttered a harsh word to her. Campbell adds:

A godly Highland minister was married to a similar woman. He sat one day in his room reading his Bible. The door opened and his wife entered. Her hand snatched the Book from him and threw it into the fire. He looked into her face and quietly made the remark, "I never sat at a warmer fire." It was an answer that turned away her wrath and marked the beginning of a new and gracious life. His Jezebel became a Lydia. The thorn became a lily.[2]

A great saint of God has said,

It is the mark of deepest and truest humility to see ourselves condemned without cause and to be silent under it. To be silent under insult and wrong is a very noble imitation of our Lord. "Oh, my Lord, when I remember in how many ways Thou didst suffer, who in no way deserved it, I know not where my senses are when I am in such haste to defend and excuse myself. Is it possible I should desire anyone to speak any good of me or to think it, when so many ill things were thought and spoken of Thee?"[3]

Repaying evil with good. An additional advance in the life of brokenness is not only to bear wrong patiently but to reward every wrong with a kindness.

Repay no one evil for evil. Have regard for good things in the sight of all men...If your enemy is hungry, feed him; if he is thirsty, give him a drink; for in so doing you will heap coals of fire on his head. Do not be overcome by evil, but overcome evil with good (Rom. 12:17, 20-21).

Here I am always reminded of the elephant that was being driven down an Indian street by its owner. The man was carrying a sharp-pointed steel goad to keep the lumbering beast moving along. Then the owner lost his grip on the goad and it fell to the ground with a resounding clang. The long-suffering elephant turned around, picked up the goad with its trunk, and held it out to the master. If elephants could be Christians, that elephant certainly was one.

Honoring others above self. This is the brand of brokenness that esteems others better than one's self (Phil. 2:3). We see it illustrated in an incident from Abram's life (Gen. 13:1-13). He and Lot had come up from Egypt to the Negev and then to Bethel with their families and possessions. Both men had extensive flocks and herds, and soon a quarrel developed between their hired hands over pasture land. It was at this point that Abram stepped in and said, in effect, "Look, Lot, we are not going to become foes over a few bales of hay. You take whatever pasturage you want, and I'll take my animals somewhere else." So Lot chose the lush pasture lands in the valley of the Jordan—ominously close to Sodom. Big-hearted Abram moved farther into Canaan. And so an Old Testament saint, living on the other side of Pentecost, gave us a practical demonstration of what Paul meant when he said, Love one another with brotherly affection; outdo one another in showing honor (Rom. 12:10).

Prompt obedience. But this is not all. God wants us to be broken in accepting and obeying His will. The psalmist puts it concisely: *"Do not be like the horse or like the mule, which have no understanding, which must be harnessed with bit and bridle, else they will not come near you"* (Ps. 32:9).

The tendency for a spirited horse is to jump the gun, whereas the mule symbolizes stubbornness and intransigence. So we have the two dangers in connection with the will of God. It is possible to move on without clear direction, to run without being sent. And then again it is possible to willfully resist the clear guidance of the Lord.

Jonah, for example. There was no question as to what God wanted him to do. He was called to go and preach repentance to Nineveh. But he was not broken as yet. So he boarded a ship going in the opposite direction. Only after his nightmarish experience in the whale's belly was his will bent to obey. Then he went forth to prove that God's will is, after all, good and acceptable and perfect (Rom. 12:2).

We get a surprising picture of brokenness in the colt which Jesus rode into Jerusalem (Lk. 19:29-35). Up to that time no man had ever ridden on that animal, and it could have been expected to vigorously resist any attempt to mount it. But when the Savior approached, it experienced a miracle of instant brokenness. The will of the colt became completely submissive to the will of its Creator.

It might be mixing metaphors to introduce clay in a discussion on brokenness, but the clay in the hands of a potter is an apt description of what a broken person is in the Lord's hands—pliable and responsive to the pressure of His fingers.

The daily prayer of the submissive saint is reflected in the words of the hymn:

157

Have Thine own way, Lord! Have Thine own way!
Thou art the Potter; I am the clay.
Mould me and make me after Thy will,
While I am waiting, yielded and still.

Have Thine own way, Lord! Have Thine own way!
Search me and try me, Master, today!
Whiter than snow, Lord, wash me just now,
As in Thy presence humbly I bow.

Have Thine own way, Lord! Have Thine own way!
Wounded and weary, help me, I pray!
Power—all power—surely is Thine!
Touch me and heal me, Savior divine!

Have Thine own way, Lord! Have Thine own way!
Hold o'er my being absolute sway!
Fill with Thy Spirit till all shall see
Christ only, always, living in me!

Death to public opinion. There are many other aspects of brokenness. For instance, we need to be brought to the place where we are dead to the world's applause or frowns. After W. P. Nicholson was saved, he came under the tutelage of a Salvation Army officer. One day the officer said to him, "If you mean business for God, wear this sign-board for a few hours in the center of town." On the board were lettered the words, "DEAD TO PUBLIC OPINION." This experience had a profound effect on all Nicholson's life of fearless service for Christ.

Confessing others' sins as our own. We need to be so

broken that we will confess the sins of God's people as our own. This is what Daniel did (Dan. 9:3-19). He was not personally guilty of most of the sins he catalogued. But he identified himself so closely with the nation of Israel that their sins became his sin. In this he reminds us, of course, of the One who "took our sins and our sorrows and made them His very own." And the lesson for us is that instead of criticizing other believers and pointing the accusing finger, we should confess their sins as if they were our own.

Keeping one's cool in crises. A final aspect of brokenness involves poise and equanimity in the crises of life. When an unavoidable delay occurs, the natural reaction is to fuss and fume. Interruptions to the regular routine often provoke annoyance and fretfulness. Mechanical breakdowns and accidents—how easily they upset us and even cause tempers to flare. Schedule changes and disappointments have a way of bringing out the worst that is in us. The frenzy, the ruffled feathers, the anger, and the hysteria that all these things arouse are ruinous to the Christian testimony, to say the least.

The way of brokenness is to keep one's cool during these crises, knowing that God is overruling all the circumstances of life for His purposes. The flat tire may be a blessing in disguise, saving you from a crash farther down the expressway. The unexpected visitor who interrupts your service for the Lord may actually present a more important ministry than what you are doing. The accident, with all its suffering, inconvenience and expense, may bring you in touch with people who have been prepared by the Holy Spirit to receive the gospel. In all these circumstances, the Lord desires to see us react instantly with calmness instead of impatience, with brokenness instead of rebellion.

These then are a few examples of what is meant by brokenness. The list is suggestive but certainly not exhaustive. As we walk in fellowship with the Lord, He will show us areas in our individual lives where we need to be broken at the foot of the Cross. And with each such revelation He will give the needed grace.

"For God is at work in you, both to will and to work for His good pleasure" (Phil. 2:13).

WHAT BROKENNESS DOES NOT MEAN

Having seen what some of the elements of brokenness are, we should explain briefly what is not meant by the word. It does not mean that the person becomes a Mr. Milquetoast, a bland, spineless sort of jellyfish. It does not mean that he becomes a powerless cipher, exerting little influence on those around him. If anything, the reverse is true. Brokenness is one of the finest elements of a strong character. It doesn't take any discipline to be unbroken. But what self control is required to be Christ-like when every natural instinct rebels against it!

Broken people are the ones with the most persuasive characters. They influence quietly by the irresistible force of an other-worldly example. It is a paradox, but there it is: *"Your gentleness has made me great"* (Ps. 18:35). And they are capable of anger when occasion demands it. We see this in the life of our Lord. He drove the money changers out of the temple with a scourge of small cords. But the important thing to see is that His anger flared not because of any wrong that was done to Him personally, but because His Father's house had been dishonored. As has been said, "He was a lion in God's cause but a lamb in His own." Many of the martyrs and reformers were truly broken but one would hardly say that they were weak or uninfluential.

THE GENERATION GAP

One of the most difficult areas in which to exercise brokenness appears to be in the child-parent relationship. By some queer quirk of fallen human nature, we seem to be most unloving to those who are closest to us. Many Christian girls wage a constant battle within themselves because of the hostility they feel toward their mothers. And just as many Christian fellows are scarcely civil to their fathers most of the time. No one denies the existence of a generation gap; actually it is an enormous gulf. The younger people complain that their parents don't understand them, that they are repressive, that they are out of touch with the times. But in spite of it all, many youth feel guilt and shame that they cannot seem to rise above these attitudes and act like Christians for a change toward their folks. They realize it is colossal defeat that they can be so kind and personable to their peers and even to other adults and yet so cold and cutting at home. They hate themselves for often wishing their parents were dead, but to break and confess is a hard pill to swallow.

It was no accident that when God gave ten basic laws to the nation of Israel, one of them should deal with this difficult and delicate area of human relations: *"Honor your father and your mother, that your days may be long upon the land which the Lord your God is giving you"* (Ex. 20:12).

Paul repeats the command in the New Testament: *"Children, obey your parents in the Lord, for this is right. Honor your father and mother, which is the first commandment with promise: that it may be well with you and you may live long on the earth"* (Eph. 6:1-3).

To honor and obey one's parents means not only to do what they say, but to respect them, to be kind to them, and to care for them whenever necessary. Paul gives four reasons: It is right. It is for the young people's own good. It is scriptural. It promotes a full life.

But many fellows and girls have almost convinced themselves that while it may be possible in other cases, it simply isn't possible in theirs. Their parents are too overbearing, too out of touch.

All that is needed is brokenness. What this will mean will be to go to the parent and say, "Look, I'm sorry that I've been such a heel in my relationships with you. I've never thanked you for all you have done for me, but I want to do it now. I want you to forgive me for the way I've built up walls of resistance between us. By God's help, I want things to be different in the future."

The timeless illustration of bridging the generation gap is the story of the prodigal son. At first the ingrate could not wait for his father to die; he wanted the inheritance right now. Well, he got it and went off to live it up.

Then followed the late-night parties, the drinks, the carousing, the sex orgies, and all the rest. But finally the money was gone and so were the friends. The wastrel was reduced to bare subsistence.

He began to think of the servants at home who were living better than he. What a fool he had been! He had left home full but now he goes back empty. He had left demanding justice but he returns pleading for mercy. He had left with head high but he crawls home broken.

"Dad," he says, "I have sinned. Sinned against God and sinned against you. I don't deserve to be your son." He had planned to say more, to plead for a job as a servant. But by this time the father was issuing orders to the household. And then before long, the son was dressed in a new suit, had a handsome ring on one finger, had a new pair of shoes on, and was sitting down to a sumptuous dinner of roast veal and all the trimmings. The gap had been bridged by brokenness. But the son would never have known the father's kiss if he had not first broken in repentance and confession.

Nothing will help to straighten out a person's attitude of hostility like the humiliation of having to make such an apology. The next time he is tempted to show any act of unlove toward a parent, he will quickly remember the scalding shame of having to break, and this will act as a powerful deterrent.

THE MARITAL GAP

Perhaps the second most difficult area in which to manifest real brokenness is in the husband-wife relationship. Once again it is a matter of acting unkindly toward those who are closest to us, while showing charm and courtesy to those we scarcely know. Too often we have to confess that we are devils at home and saints abroad.

The Bible is realistic in anticipating the possibility of tension in the marriage relationship. We think especially of Colossians 3:19: *"Husbands, love your wives and do not be bitter toward them."*

The bitterness that can develop in a husband toward his wife is often so deep that he despairs of ever rising above it. Too often he simply gives up and seeks release through separation or divorce. Take the case of Jano and Jinx. The first time they met, they both knew they were meant for each other. During the months that followed they were together at every opportunity. By the end of six months they were engaged, and the wedding was set for six months later. But as things turned out, they were married four months after their engagement.

The wedding went off with everyone playing his part in the little game quite well. And for the first year things went fairly smoothly. Then one day they had a violent quarrel and Jinx released all her suppressed disrespect of Jano for what had happened before their marriage. He repaid her in kind. The walls quivered and the windows bulged. After that it seemed that their marriage was in hopeless ruins. Jano found that the bitterness he felt toward his wife was greater than the love with which he had loved her (2 Sam. 13:15).

Friends suggested that they see a Christian marriage counselor, and they did. But underneath they were as hard and unyielding as the bars of a castle.

Finally Jano applied for a divorce. But before the case came up in court, a Christian friend challenged him to try the way of brokenness. And the friend's wife reached Jinx at the same time with the same message. Why not break before the Lord and before one another? Why not put the past under the blood of Christ and make a new start?

They did. It was the hardest thing that either had ever done. But they got together and made a complete confession. There was no hedging or self-vindication. It was as forthright a confession as one could wish for. Each one accepted responsibility for his part in their pre-marital sin. After tearful confession to the Lord, they covenanted never to reproach one another with this sin again. They claimed the promise of God that they had been forgiven (1 Jn. 1:9). They gladly forgave each other for everything. And each one decided that he must also forgive himself. When they rose from their knees, an enormous burden had been lifted. They realized that there would still be a period of adjustment, but the nuclear cloud of bitterness and strife had dissipated. And they realized the necessity for continual brokenness whenever future problems would arise in the home.

Months later Jano put down the evening paper and commented how strange it was that people would spend time and money at marriage counselors and psychiatrists, and try any form of expensive "treatment," but they would not try the way of brokenness. And yet without brokenness, the other things were largely ineffective.

It is not only in family relationships, but in all areas of our life the Lord wants us to be broken. He will wrestle with us as He wrestled with Jacob at Peniel. He will try to break us of pride, of self-will, of an unforgiving spirit, of stubbornness, of gossip, of backbiting, of worldliness, of impurity, of temper, of every work of the flesh. He wants to change our name from Jacob to Israel, from cheat to prince, from powerless schemer to one who has power with God and man. He will wrestle with us till the breaking of the day and put our thigh out of joint. Then we will go through the rest of our life with the limp of a broken man whom God can use.

God wants us to be blameless. None of us is sinless but we can all be blameless. A blameless person is one who, when he does commit some wrong, is quick to make it right. He does not let the sun go down on his wrath. By confession and apology, he keeps the lines of communication open with God and with his fellow men. An elder in a local church must be blameless (1 Tim. 3:2), but every Christian should be.

THINK OF THE RESULTS

Think what it would mean in our individual lives, in our homes, in the local church and in the business world if we were all broken as we should be.

In our own lives it would mean greater power, greater

happiness, and better health. The men who have the greatest spiritual impact on others are those who are yoked with Christ in meekness and humility. They are the ones who find fulfillment and rest in serving Him. And what is good for us spiritually is good for our physical health as well. The *British Medical Journal* once reported that "there is not a tissue in the human body wholly removed from the spirit." Dr. Paul Tournier tells of a patient who had had anemia for months. Then it mysteriously disappeared and her blood was normal again. Investigation revealed that she had had a spiritual crisis, namely, she had forgiven a long-standing grudge.[1] Yes, brokenness is good for the health.

Think of a home where the members keep short accounts with one another. Of course, there are differences from time to time, but they are not allowed to build up steam in the boiler. The family has learned the holy art of kissing and making up. That is the kind of home where Jesus loves to be.

In the local assembly, brokenness is the road to revival. It is a fixed law in the spiritual realm that the tears of brokenness are the prelude to showers of blessing. We generally try everything else first—new buildings, new campaigns, new methods, but God is waiting for repentance and humiliation. When we repent the blessing will flow.

If My people who are called by My name will humble themselves, and pray and seek My face, and turn from their wicked ways, then I will hear from heaven, and will forgive their sin and heal their land (2 Chron. 7:14).

Think of the impact that Christians would have in the business world by exhibiting brokenness. Men of the world are not broken and they like to pit their strength against others who are like them. But they are nonplussed when they bump into someone who doesn't react with anger, who admits wrong and apologizes, who exhibits the grace of the Lord Jesus. It is this supernatural kind of life that speaks loudly for Christ in the rough and tumble world of commerce today.

LORD, BREAK ME!

Some years ago, in a missionary prayer meeting, I heard an earnest young believer pray, "Lord, break me!" The request jarred me. Up to that time in my life, I had never prayed that prayer. And I wasn't sure I was ready to pray it even then. But those words, flowing hissing hot from the heart of that young disciple, awakened me to the tremendous need of brokenness in my own life. They created an awareness that this was a fantastically vital area in the spiritual realm. And now they have become the constant prayer of an aspiring heart: *"LORD, BREAK ME!"*

ENDNOTES

Terms of Discipleship

1. H. A. Evan Hopkins, *Henceforth*, Chicago: IVF, 1954, p. 20.

Forsaking All

1. "Men of His Right Hand," *Witness Magazine,* January 1961.

2. A. N. Groves, *Christian Devotedness,* Kansas City: Walterick Publishers, 1975.

3. Norman Grubb, *C. T. Studd,* London: Lutterworth Press, 1957, p. 64.

4. Elisabeth Elliot, *Shadow of the Almighty,* New York: Harper & Brothers, 1958, p. 246.

5. *Christian Devotedness*, op. cit., pp. 26-27.

6. G. H. Lang, *Anthony Norris Groves,* London: The Paternoster Press, 1949, p. 54.

7. *Christian Devotedness*, op. cit., p. 35 (footnote).

Zeal

1. Norman Grubb, *C. T. Studd,* London: Lutterworth Press, 1957, p. 36.

2. Elisabeth Elliot, *Shadow of the Almighty,* New York: Harper & Brothers, 1958, pp. 58-59.

3. Quoted by Billy Graham in Mission Commitment, Part 1, message given at InterVarsity Christian Fellowship Conference, Urbana IL, 1957. Theme of conference: One Lord, One Church, One World.

4. J. C. Ryle, *Practical Religion,* London: James Clarke & Co. Ltd., 1959, p.130.

Faith

1. C. H. Mackintosh, *Genesis to Deuteronomy,* Neptune, NJ: Loizeaux Brothers, 1972, p. 498

2. C. H. Mackintosh, *The Mackintosh Treasury,* Neptune, NJ: Loizeaux Brothers, 1976.

World Dominion

1. C. H. Spurgeon, quoted in *The Prairie Overcomer,* Three Hills, Alberta: Prairie Bible Institute, March 1957, p. 81.

Discipleship and Marriage

1. Gordon Arnold Lonsdale, *TIME magazine,* Feb. 17, 1961.

2. Wesley L. Gustafson, *Called But Not Going,* Chicago: IVCF Press, p. 10.

3. Cable & French, *Ambassadors For Christ,* Chicago: Moody Press, n.d.

The Shadow of Martyrdom

1. Elisabeth Elliot, *Shadow of the Almighty,* New York: Harper & Brothers, 1958, p. 240.

ENDNOTES

What's the Harm in It?

1. Frederick A. Filby, quoted in *Creation Revealed,* London: Pickering & Inglis Ltd., 1964, p. 126.

2. Samuel Cox, *St. Paul and His Converts*

3. J. C. Ryle, *Practical Religion,* London: James Clarke & Co., 1959.

The Case for Frozen Assets

1. J. R. Miller, "Come Ye Apart," *New Englander and Yale Review,* Volume 48, Issue 219, June 1888.

God Values Broken Things

1. R. C. H. Lenski, *St. Paul's Epistles to the Galatians, Ephesians & Philippians,* Minneapolis, MN: Augsburg Publishing House, 1937, p. 588.

2. Murdoch Campbell, *From Grace to Glory,* London: Banner of Truth Trust, 1970, p. 149.

3. J. Allen Blair, *Living Patiently,* Neptune, NJ: Loizeaux Brothers, n.d., pp. 353-354.

God Wants Us All to Be Broken

1. Dr. Paul Tournier, *A Doctor's Casebook in the Light of the Bible* (Trans. Edwin Hudson), New York: Harper and Brothers, 1960.

STUDY GUIDE
TO
TRUE DISCIPLESHIP

based on William MacDonald's *True Discipleship*

Anthony Payne

FOREWORD

$\mathcal{T}$his Study Guide consists of twelve lessons designed for use with the three sections of this book: True Discipleship, Where is Your Treasure? and Lord, Break Me! Its purpose is to help a Christian explore for himself some of the principles of discipleship set forth in the New Testament. MacDonald's book then serves as a commentary which the student uses to supplement his own personal study of the Scriptures.

These studies may be used profitably in any of three ways:

1. *Personal study:* For each lesson, the student should complete his study as directed. The lesson will indicate when and where to read in MacDonald's book. Each lesson should require about one hour to complete.

2. *One-on-one discipling:* Those engaged in the work of helping others to grow in the faith may assign these studies to those they are discipling and then discuss with them the principles learned.

3. *Bible study groups:* These studies are suitable for a 12- or 13-week class. Each student should do his own study

beforehand and come prepared to discuss his findings. A class session of one hour is more than adequate for discussion. If the discussion is limited to thirty minutes, the remainder of the session may be used in other ways. For example, the class leader may expound on aspects of the lesson, or the class may spend time in prayer for the needs of the students, the church, the unsaved, etc. The class may also be assigned book reports of supplementary reading on the subject of discipleship, and these reports may be discussed.

CONTENTS

Lesson One

TERMS OF DISCIPLESHIP

1. What did Jesus mean by His statement in Luke 14:26? Why is it impossible to be His disciple without complying with this statement?

2. Matthew 16:24 gives three requirements for one who wishes to be Jesus' disciple. Identify and give a brief definition of each. Then cite specific examples of how a believer might violate each requirement.

3. What characteristics of a disciple does Jesus give in John 13:35? In your opinion, how does it show others that we are His disciples?

4. Explain the importance of the Scriptures in the life of a true disciple (Jn. 8:31). What attitude will he have toward the Word of God?

5. What must a disciple of the Lord Jesus do according to Luke 14:33? If you did this, how specifically would your life change? What benefits would be derived from obeying Jesus in this area?

✎ *Read "Terms of Discipleship" (pp. 11-16) before answering questions 6 and 7.*

6. For each statement below, state whether you agree or disagree and then give your reasons:

• "True Christianity is an all-out commitment to the Lord Jesus Christ."

• "Nothing less than unconditional surrender could ever be a fitting response to His sacrifice at Calvary."

• "…we have every right to enjoy the best that this life has to offer."

7. List the seven terms of discipleship brought out in questions 1-5. Which of these is hardest for you to accept? In light of Christ's claims upon you, how will you seek from now on to be a true disciple?

Lesson Two

FORSAKING ALL

1. What condition of discipleship does the Lord Jesus set forth in Luke 14:33? What does He mean by His statement?

2. Study Matthew 6:19-21 and Luke 12:33-34. What does the Lord command His disciples? Contrast the two places where we can lay up treasure. What is the relationship between the place we accumulate treasure and our devotion to God?

3. How did the believers in the early Church obey Jesus' commands (Acts 2:44-45)?

✎ *Before completing questions 4 and 5, read "Forsaking All" (pp. 17-25).*

4. Consider each of the following arguments against taking the words of the Lord literally. In your own words, refute each argument and cite scriptures supporting your reasoning.

• "If we forsook all, we would starve."

• "We must provide for the future needs of our families."

• "If every Christian forsook all, then who would finance the work of the Lord?"

• "If there were no wealthy Christians, then who would reach the higher class of people with the gospel?"

5. Study the four characteristics (listed in the book) of the man who forsakes all. To what extent is each true of your own life?

6. What does it mean **for you** to *"forsake all"* to follow Christ? State your answer in personal and practical terms.

7. If you took the words of Jesus in Luke 14:33 literally, what would be the practical impact on each of the areas below? Be specific.

• Your job/education

• Your family life

• Your church

• The world

Lesson Three

HINDRANCES TO DISCIPLESHIP

1. Study Luke 9:57-62 and identify the three would-be disciples of Jesus. What does the first man volunteer to do (v. 57)? How does the Lord reply (v. 58)? Why do you think He replies in this way?

2. What does the Lord command the second man (v. 59)? What request does the man then make? What does Jesus mean when He says, *"Let the dead bury their dead"*? What does He say should take priority?

3. What condition does the third man place upon following Jesus (v. 61)? What is wrong with his request? What makes a man not *"fit for the kingdom of God"*?

4. How are the three men alike? How are they different? The last two men both used the words, *"Lord...me first..."* What does this tell you about them? How are their words contradictory?

5. Read "Hindrances to Discipleship" (pp. 27-32). Identi-

fy the names given to the men. Why is each name fitting?

6. What three primary hindrances to true discipleship do these men illustrate? Give specific examples of how these hindrances might occur in your life.

7. What comes between you and complete devotion to the Lord Jesus Christ? What steps will you take to remove these hindrances?

Lesson Four

DISCIPLES ARE STEWARDS

Study carefully Luke 16:1-13 and answer the following questions:

1. To whom is the Lord Jesus speaking? In your own words, summarize the parable that He tells (vv. 1-8a).

2. What motivated the unjust steward's actions (vv. 3-4)? In your opinion, why did the rich man think that his steward acted wisely (v. 8a)?

3. Consider our Lord's statement in verse 8b. Who are the *"sons of this world"* and the *"sons of light"*? Contrast their views of the future. Why does the Lord say that the sons of this world are wiser than the sons of light?

4. List ways in which people today prepare for their future. According to the Lord, how should a disciple prepare for his future (v. 9)? What is the *"mammon of unrighteousness"*? How can you use it to *"make friends"* for yourself? Be specific.

5. How is the way in which we deal with possessions a test of our character (v. 10)? In practical terms, what does it mean for a Christian to be *"faithful"* in small matters? To be *"unjust"* in small matters?

6. What are *"true riches"* (v. 11)? What is the prerequisite for being entrusted with them? What do you think really belongs to a Christian (v. 12)? What is required to receive it? What principle of service does the Lord give (v. 13)? How is this related to stewardship?

✎ *Read "Disciples are Stewards" (pp. 33-38) and record additional insights into questions 1-6.*

7. Based on this study, explain **why** a disciple of Christ is a steward and **how** he is to exercise that stewardship. What changes do you need to make in the way you manage God's interests here on earth? What will be the spiritual and eternal results?

Lesson Five

ZEAL AND FAITH

1. Look up the word "zeal" in a dictionary and write a brief definition in your own words. In your opinion, how should this word apply to a disciple of the Lord Jesus?

2. How did the Lord Jesus' life on earth manifest zeal (Lk. 12:50; Jn. 2:17; 9:4)?

3. Read the chapter entitled "Zeal" (pp. 39-46). Explain each of the following statements:

• "A zealous man in religion is pre-eminently a man of one thing."

• "The disgrace of the Church in the twentieth century is that more zeal is evident among Communists and cultists than among Christians."

• "If the Lord Jesus is worth anything, He is worth everything."

4. Read the chapter called "Faith" (pp. 47-52) and identify at least five major principles pertaining to a life of faith.

5. In practical terms, contrast walking *"by faith"* and walking *"by sight"* (2 Cor. 5:7).

6. How can a disciple increase in faith?

7. What things in your life cause your zeal for Christ to diminish? What positive adjustments do you need to make to increase in zeal? To what degree would you say that you *"walk by faith and not by sight"*? What changes do you need to make to walk more by faith?

Lesson Six

PRAYER

✎ *Read the chapter on "Prayer" (pp. 53-60), study carefully the principles of prayer, and then answer the following questions in your own words.*

1. Why does the best prayer come from a strong inward necessity? List some reasons why our prayer life tends to be shallow.

2. What does it mean to *"draw near with a true heart"* (Heb. 10:22)? What are some ways that we tend to be hypocritical in our prayers?

3. What are some of the ways in which prayer costs us something? Why do you think that God honors this kind of prayer? What relationship does fasting have to prayer?

4. How can prayer be used wrongly (Jas. 4:3)? What should be the primary burden of prayer? How can we honor God through prayer?

5. Explain what it means to pray in the *"name of the Lord Jesus."*

6. What is the importance of each of the following to prayer?

- "keeping short accounts with God"

- "abiding in Christ"

- "praying specifically"

7. Write a paragraph describing the place of prayer in your life as a disciple of Christ. Which of the principles of prayer mentioned in the book *True Discipleship* do you neglect most? What steps are you taking to become more effective in prayer?

Lesson Seven

WARFARE

1. In what kind of conflict are the disciples of the Lord Jesus involved (Eph. 6:11-12)? What strategy does the enemy use (2 Cor. 11:14-15)? In your opinion, why is a knowledge of the enemy and his strategy important?

2. What are the weapons of the Christian warfare (Eph. 6:13-20)? Describe the effectiveness of these weapons (2 Cor. 10:3-5). How are you proving their effectiveness in your daily life?

3. Study 2 Timothy 2:3-4. What does Paul urge Timothy to do (v. 3)? What is the characteristic of a soldier in active service (v. 4)? List ways in which the Christian soldier can be *"entangled."* Which of these is the greatest threat to you?

4. What problems arise in an army if the soldiers lack unity? Why is disunity a serious problem in the Christian warfare? Read Philippians 2 and identify key principles regarding the way to achieve unity. Give examples of how you can apply these.

5. Why is sacrificial living necessary in times of war? Why is it equally important in the Christian warfare? What sacrifices is the Christian soldier called upon to make?

6. Read the chapter entitled "Warfare" (pp. 61-67) and record any additional insights on questions 1-5. Identify the eight demands of war and write a sentence summarizing why each is a demand of the Christian warfare.

7. What practices in your life indicate that you take seriously the Christian warfare? What is your strategy for becoming a more effective soldier of Jesus Christ?

Lesson Eight

WORLD DOMINION

1. Study Matthew 28:18-20, Mark 16:15, and 2 Corinthians 5:18-20. In what sense has Christ called His disciples to world dominion?

2. What must be the motive if the world is to be reached for Christ (Mt. 22:37, 39; 1 Cor. 13:1-3; 2 Cor. 5:14-15)? Why is this the only adequate motive? How did the apostle Paul reflect this motive (Acts 20:24; 2 Cor. 12:15a)?

3. What method did the early disciples use to reach the world with the gospel (Mk. 16:15, 20; Acts 8:4)? Where would you expect to find them proclaiming the gospel?

4. What is another method of propagating the Christian faith (Mk. 3:14; 2 Tim. 2:2)? In your opinion, why is this method just as important as the public proclamation of the gospel?

✎ *Read the chapter on "World Dominion" (pp. 69-77) before completing questions 5 and 6.*

5. Explain the following statements:

• "It was never God's intention that we should be 'born a man and die a grocer.'"

• "The Christian's calling is the noblest of all, and if we realize it, our lives will take on a new loftiness."

6. Identify the six basic principles cited in *True Discipleship* that disciples follow as they go forth to proclaim Christ to the world.

7. God has called us to world dominion. What is your response? Write a paragraph explaining how this call practically affects your life. How are you personally involved in the two principal methods of reaching the world with the gospel?

Lesson Nine

DISCIPLESHIP AND MARRIAGE

1. Why did God institute marriage for the human race?

- Genesis 1:28
- Genesis 2:18
- 1 Corinthians 7:2

2. What is God's view of marriage?

- Proverbs 18:22
- Hebrews 13:4a

Consider Ecclesiastes 4:9-12. What benefits can marriage bring to a disciple's labor for the Lord? Based on the results of your study so far, write a paragraph explaining why marriage is not incompatible with a life of purity, devotion, and service for Christ.

3. Study Matthew 19:10-12. Identify the three situations in which a person might forego marriage. What does it mean to be a *"[eunuch] for the kingdom of heaven's sake"* (v. 12)?

✎ *Read 1 Corinthians 7 carefully before answering questions 4-7.*

4. The apostle Paul expresses the wish that the unmarried remain as he was, that is, unmarried (1 Cor. 7:7a, 8). List all the reasons he gives for celibacy in 1 Corinthians 7:26-35. Is Paul therefore telling the saints that they are out of God's will or "less spiritual" if they marry? Explain your answer.

5. What determines whether a Christian should remain celibate (1 Cor. 7:7b; Mt. 19:12)? How does one know if he is able to remain unmarried (1 Cor. 7:9)?

6. How should married Christians live (1 Cor. 7:29-31)? In practical terms, what will this mean?

✎ *Read "Discipleship and Marriage" (pp. 79-83). Record any additional thoughts on questions 1-6.*

7. In what ways might marriage be a bitter enemy of God's purposes for your life?

• *For the unmarried:* What major principles will guide you in determining whether God has called you to married life or to celibacy?

• *For the married:* What changes are needed in your family life to secure greater devotion to Christ and His cause?

Lesson Ten

COUNTING THE COST,
REAPING THE REWARDS

✎ *Carefully read Luke 14:25-35 and then answer questions 1-4.*

1. What does Jesus demand from all who would be His disciples?

> • verse 26

> • verse 27

2. Identify the two parables that Jesus uses in verses 28-32. Summarize each. Then state the aspect of the Christian life each parable illustrates, and finally summarize its main spiritual lesson. You may lay it out in chart form:

	Summary	Likeness to Christian Life	Lesson
vv. 28-30			
vv. 31-32			

In what way do these parables illustrate the demands of verses 26-27?

3. How is verse 33 an application to all that Jesus has said in verses 26-32?

4. Consider verses 34-35. What does *"salt"* refer to in a figurative sense? What is Jesus really saying about discipleship in the figure of the salt? How might a Christian lose his *"savor"*?

✎ *Read the chapter on "Counting the Cost" (pp. 85-89). Record any additional insights into questions 1-4.*

5. Study John 12:23-26. What fundamental principle does Jesus illustrate with wheat (v. 24)? How did this principle apply to the Lord Jesus? How should the principle apply to His disciples? What will be the reward?

6. Read "The Shadow of Martyrdom" and "The Rewards of True Discipleship" (pp. 91-97). For each statement below, state whether you agree or disagree, and give your reasons:

• "When a man is truly committed to Jesus Christ, it seems to be a matter of no importance to him whether he lives or dies."

• "Not all are required to lay down their lives as martyrs.... But each of us can have the martyr spirit, the martyr zeal, the martyr devotion."

• "…the life of true discipleship is the most spiritually satisfying life in the world…."

7. How has the Lord Jesus challenged you personally to count the cost of being His disciple? List the obstacles in your life which hinder complete devotion to Christ and the actions you intend to take to overcome these obstacles.

Lesson Eleven

WHERE IS YOUR TREASURE?

1. Study Matthew 6:19-21. What does the Lord Jesus forbid His followers to do? Explain the meaning of verse 21 in practical terms.

2. What do the apostle Paul's example and his instruction teach about diligence in business (Acts 18:1-3; 2 Thess. 3:8, 10)? Consider the statement: "A Christian may earn as much money as he can." Under what conditions is this true?

- Proverbs 13:11
- Proverbs 22:16
- Psalm 62:10
- Matthew 6:24
- Matthew 6:33
- 1 Timothy 5:8

3. What is God's will concerning our use of riches?

- Matthew 6:19-21
- 1 Timothy 6:6-8
- 1 Corinthians 4:1-2
- 1 Timothy 6:17-19

Why is it wrong for a Christian to hoard riches?

- Proverbs 3:27-28
- Malachi 3:8
- 1 John 3:17

✎ *Read "Where is Your Treasure?" (pp. 101-119) and record any additional insights on questions 1-3.*

4. Nine arguments used to justify hoarding riches for the future are cited in the section "The Case for Frozen Assets" (pp. 121-130). Select one of these arguments, summarize it, and give an answer to it in your own words.

5. Identify some of the perils of riches.

- Proverbs 28:20, 22
- Matthew 6:24
- Matthew 19:23-26
- 1 Timothy 6:9-10
- James 1:10-11
- James 5:1-6

6. Re-read the sections "A Warning to the Lazy" and "A Warning Against Judging" (pp. 138-139). State how each of these warnings apply personally to you.

7. How can you make this lesson practical in your own life? State specific steps that you will take.

Lesson Twelve

LORD, BREAK ME!

1. Contrast God's attitude toward a broken man with His attitude toward a proud man (Ps. 34:18; 51:17; 138:6; Isa. 57:15; Jas. 4:6).

2. Why is conversion a form of brokenness? Study Matthew 11:28-30. What is a yoke? Why are yokes only for those who are broken? What is the meaning of the Lord's statement here?

3. How did true brokenness manifest itself in the life of each of the following men?

> • David (Ps. 32:3-5)
> • Daniel (Dan. 9:3-19)
> • Zacchaeus (Lk. 19:1-10)
> • The Lord Jesus (1 Pet. 2:23)

4. What are some of the basic elements of brokenness brought to our attention by the following verses?

- Matthew 18:23-35; Ephesians 4:32
- Romans 12:17, 20, 21
- Philippians 2:3; Romans 12:10
- Psalm 32:8-9

5. Read "Lord, Break Me!" (pp. 140-168) and identify the ten elements of brokenness mentioned. Which of these are seen in the life of Christ as depicted in Philippians 2:6-8? Explain. Your observation may be laid out in chart form as follows:

Element of brokenness	How it is seen in Christ

6. Which elements of brokenness are most difficult for you to exhibit in the areas listed below? Explain your answer.

- in your home
- in your church
- on your job

7. Identify specific attitudes or actions in your daily life that demonstrate a lack of brokenness. What will you do about these? Be specific.